An Introduction to

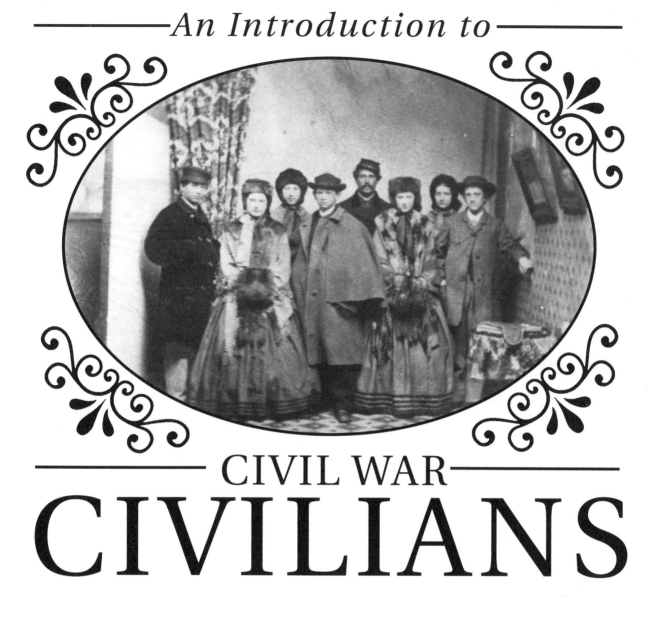

CIVIL WAR
CIVILIANS

Juanita Leisch

THOMAS PUBLICATIONS
Gettysburg PA 17325

Copyright © 1994 Juanita Leisch

Printed in the United States of America.

Published by THOMAS PUBLICATIONS
PO Box 3031
Gettysburg, PA 17325

ISBN-0-939631-70-9

Cover design by Ryan C. Stouch

Photo Credits:

Illinois State Historical Library: p. 78.

Library of Congress: pp. 26 (top), 54, 58 (top), 64, 67 (bottom).

Private Collections: pp. Front cover, 1, 2, 3, 4, 5, 6, 7, 9, 10, 11, 12, 13, 14, 15, 16, 17, 18, 19, 20, 21, 22, 23, 24, 25, 26 (bottom), 27, 28, 29, 30, 32, 33, 34, 35, 36, 37, 38, 40, 42, 43, 47 (bottom), 49, 52 (bottom), 53 (top), 55 (top, right & bottom), 61 (bottom), 62, 63, 65, 68, 69 (top), 70, 72 (right), 79, 80, 81, Inside back cover, Back cover.

U.S. Army Military History Institute: pp. iv, v, 8, 31, 39, 41, 44, 45, 46, 47 (top), 48, 50, 51, 52 (top), 53 (bottom), 55 (top, left), 57, 58 (bottom), 59, 61 (top), 66, 67 (top), 69 (bottom), 71, 72 (left), 73, 74, 76.

Table of Contents

Preface

The ruins of downtown Richmond, Virginia. This photograph was taken at about the time that Judith White Brockenbrough McGuire left Richmond to live with her brother in Winchester, Virginia.

By reciting the words in a low, unwavering voice, she willed herself to be calm.

> Last night, (it seems strange that we have lived to speak or write of it,) between nine and ten o'clock...we were startled by the rapid firing of cannon. At first we thought that there must be an attack upon the city...but the firing was too regular....We threw up the windows, and saw the flashes and smoke of cannon....What could it be? We called to passers-by: "What do those guns mean?" At last a voice wickedly replied: "General Lee has surrendered, thank God!" Of course we did not believe him....[1]

Judith White Brockenbrough McGuire sat at a borrowed desk in her brother's house, reading from her own journal. She'd kept it so that her grandchildren might understand "Why." Why—they would never see her lovely home in Alexandria. Why—they would live in near-poverty, when their grandparents had once been so comfortable. Why—so many things had changed. The journal had fallen open to the entry for April 10—the first night of the hundred gun salutes in Richmond. She continued reading, letting the events unfold again.

> Again we called out: "What is the matter?" A voice answered, as if from a broken heart: "They say General Lee has surrendered." We cannot believe it....At day-break the dreadful salute commenced again....Another hundred—can it be so?

She turned the page, and looked away, composing herself. She consciously searched for more pleasant thoughts: oh yes—there was her brother's generosity. He had helped her find employment as a school teacher, even in those difficult times. She smiled and thought about him introducing her to the children. Her eyes cleared, and she was able to continue reading the almost-daily entries in her journal.

> Fearful rumours are reaching us...that it is all too true, and that General Lee surrendered on Sunday last, the 9th of April....We do not yet give up all hope. General Johnston is in the field....

Strange rumours are afloat to-night. It is said, and believed, that Lincoln is dead, and Seward much injured...the story is strengthened by the way which the Yankees treat it....I trust that, if true, it may not be by the hand of an assassin, though it would seem to fulfil the warnings of the Scripture....

For ourselves, like the rest of the refugees, we are striving to get from the city....The Northern officials offer free tickets to persons returning to their homes—alas! to their homes! How few of us have homes! Some are confiscated, others are destroyed.

She shifted in the unfamiliar chair, and propped her forehead in her hand as she turned the page to read her last two entries for the month of April, 1865.

J.P arrived to-day direct from Mosby's command, which is disbanded, but has not surrendered. He is full of enthusiasm...and is bent on joining Johnston. Dear boy, his hopeful spirit has infected me, and aroused a hope which I am afraid to indulge....
...Dear M., in her sadness, has put some Confederate money, and postage stamps into a Confederate envelope, sealed it up, and endorsed it, "In memory of our beloved Confederacy." I feel like doing the same, and treasuring up the buttons, and the stars, and the dear gray coats, faded and worn as they are, with the soiled and tattered banner, the untarnished sword and other arms, though defeated, still crowned with glory. But not yet—I cannot feel that all is over yet.

She read the last line again. "yet—I cannot feel that all is over yet." Her eyes filled with tears. She pressed her lips together, and blinked several times. Without taking her eyes off the paper, she picked up the pen and made the final entry in her wartime journal.

May 4
General Johnston surrendered on the 26th of April. "My native land, good-night!"

When Judith McGuire recorded the death of Abraham Lincoln, saying: "I trust that, if true, it may not be by the hand of an assassin, though it would seem to fulfil the warnings of the Scripture..." she apparently thought the biblical reference was so obvious that she did not even bother to record it. What biblical prophesy foretold the assassination of Abraham Lincoln?

Today, many Americans would be hard-pressed to name that—or many other—unfulfilled biblical prophecies. This difference is just one example of the way in which American culture has changed since the Civil War.

The Presidential Booth at Ford's Theater, site of Abraham Lincoln's assassination. Judith White Brockenbrough McGuire stated in her diary that the assassination fulfilled a biblical prophecy.

It is also an example of the difficulty modern Americans have in understanding the actions and reactions of those who lived during the Civil War. There are distinct (if subtle) differences between the culture of modern readers and that of the Americans who lived at the time of the Civil War. The modern reader must have some knowledge of mid-nineteenth century Americans in order to understand them.

This book introduces many of the concepts necessary to understanding mid-nineteenth century Americans, and their involvement in the Civil War. Specifically, it provides basic information on individuals, their families, and the society and communities in which they lived. After laying this basis, the text describes issues of everyday life and how individual, family, and community standards were reflected in the military. It examines the ways in which civilians participated in the war, and the ways in which the war changed the lives of American civilians.

Acknowledgements

There have been times when I wondered if I could really write this book, and it is only by the grace of God and with the help of many people that this book has become a reality. I would like to mention just a few of the many individuals who should receive credit for inspiring anything which is admirable in this book. For any inaccuracies, I alone am responsible.

First, I'd like to thank Les Jensen, my best friend, my critic. His comments and his knowledge of military history led me to many of the analogies in this book. Les continued to listen and to talk to me about this book long after others would run at the mere mention of it.

Chris Nelson, Harris Andrews, Ann Gates, and Harry Roach provided the early inspiration and impetus for this book. Jerry Coates and Don Troiani gave me encouragement when the project faltered.

Nan McGavock, Kate Hanley, Linda Livingstone and Joan Porter formed a focus group, and provided me with the tough realities of an unpredictable audience. George Glaros graciously agreed to edit the book, providing a fresh perspective, and a professional's influence.

For the visual information in the book, I am indebted to Gil Barrett, Henry Deeks, Linda Duffy, H.M. Madaus, Ted Twardowski and Mike O'Donnell.

One source of information for this book, Janet Nash, embodies all that an aspiring writer could hope for. When I contacted her about her ancestor, Robert Smalls, she opened her home and her archives to me. The world can't be all bad when there are caring, concerned people like Janet Nash to preserve the artifacts of our past.

I also want to thank John Beamer, Jeff Copeland, and Val Collins for sharing their family stories with me.

Like so many other researchers, I have skimmed the surface of the information which is maintained in the National Archives and the Library of Congress. The evening staffs of those two institutions are surely the unsung heroes of Washington, DC. I also took advantage of the endless patience and assistance that is provided to researchers who visit the photo archives at the U.S. Army Military History Institute at Carlisle Barracks, PA. Mike Winey, Randy Hackenburg, and Geffery Hoskins embody the sort of helpfulness and fonts of information which make the difference between struggling and enjoying historical research.

Dean Thomas (publisher) and Mary Hush (editor) of this book are the most patient people in the world. No writer could ask for a better publisher.

Kate Hanley, who did the design, adds beauty and understanding to every person's life, or project, that she touches.

John Corgan and Jim Thomas did the layout work on this book, sitting in front of a computer screen for days, weeks, hours, scanning pictures and deciphering thousands of illegible notes. Thanks!

Finally, and most importantly, I want to thank my mom and dad, Mr. and Mrs. Joseph Leisch, Jr., who deserve much credit for instigating and nurturing my interest in this topic. I must also thank them for never letting me forget that this project needed my attention. They never stopped believing that I could, would, (and should) finish it.

Chapter I
Mid 19th Century America

Individuals

Many modern Americans consider themselves to be "basically good," and do not spend time berating themselves for being "sinful." Americans of the mid-nineteenth century might have disagreed. One key characteristic of mid-nineteenth century Americans was an adherence to strict individual ethics. Most people lived their daily lives in constant confrontation with "good" and "evil." Often, they had daily and personal involvement in religious practices.

Make no mistake, there was crime and unethical behavior in mid-nineteenth century America. The difference between this culture and that of modern Americans lies not so much in what people actually did (and still do), but in what was expected of them: Americans were expected to have a well-defined and consistent sense of right and wrong. From infancy, mid-nineteenth century Americans were bombarded with moral teachings. Writers of children's books tried to teach morals and ethics. Entertainment was a secondary goal. Children were taught that right was right, and wrong was wrong, even if wrong was done for a good cause.

The lesson that ethics were absolute—and did not change depending on the situation—was applied in day-to-day lives of adults as well as children. Non-situational ethics meant, for example, that law cases were more often settled on the factual point of whether a crime was committed than whether the crime was justified, or the criminal was capable of distinguishing right from wrong.

From infancy, mid-nineteenth century Americans were bombarded with moral teachings.

Another attitude shared by most mid-nineteenth century Americans was the tendency to set very long-term goals, and to live life with those goals in mind. Religions emphasized the afterlife, and many Americans lived life with a view to their eternal future. Today, Americans value good health, and those who wish to discourage the use of alcohol and tobacco argue that they lead to diseases. In the mid-nineteenth century, opinion holders kept in mind the view of the long-term: They argued that these habits were evil vices which led down the path to hell. Everlasting damnation was a far more compelling argument than the threat of physical illness.

The most mundane incidents—even those which would seem merely comical today—brought to mind religious images. Ruthie Osgood was a typical young

BROTHER AND SISTER.

FOOTBALL is a game for boys, though a gentle brother and sister may sometimes play it, rather than have no sport in the open air. And when boys play it by themselves, they must not be rude and brutal. You can do to others as you wish them to do to you, even in the midst of a hot and eager game of football.

HOME, SWEET HOME.

How gladly we get safely back to it, from a journey; and still more if we come home from long banishment, fully forgiven and welcome! How dear are home comforts, home peace, and love. We are exiles from heaven; but God has a glorious home for us there, and if we come to him in Christ, he will see us afar off, and welcome us.

Writers of children's books tried to teach morals and ethics. Entertainment was a secondary goal.

woman, writing frequent letters to her brother, Charlie who was away at war. In the letters, she kept Charlie updated about the details of life in their small Massachusetts community:

> ...Last night when we were going down the icy street there was a man just ahead of us, when all of a sudden down he went, pretty much as I imagine Satan did and I should judge by the way he went along holding on behind it hurt him some....[2]

God and Satan were everywhere. It was common practice for mid-nineteenth century Americans to credit both good and bad events to divine intervention—be it providence or punishment. In modern times, Americans use malpractice suits to determine when doctors are not sufficiently skilled to do their job. In the mid-nineteenth century, Americans credited God with determining the success or failure of medical treatments, trusting that even a bad doctor could bring good health if God willed it.

In the Civil War, when soldiers survived fierce battles, they attributed their safety not to their own skill—or their enemy's lack thereof—but rather to the will of God.

Lithographs with religious themes were mass-produced and sold, so that families could insert them in their family albums, or frame them and display them in the home.

This full-plate ambrotype shows the interior of a church with a minister and choir in place. It would be extremely unusual for a photograph to be taken during an actual church service, therefore, this picture was probably posed.

Families

Contrary to modern myths about the past, the mid-nineteenth century household seldom consisted of a simple nuclear family; mother, father and children. "Setting up housekeeping" or "keeping house" was a full time occupation, and elderly and single adults often lived with family members instead of keeping house for themselves.

This also gave adults who became widows or widowers an added incentive to remarry. Second—and third—marriages were not at all uncommon. It is incorrect to believe that half-siblings, step-mothers, and single-parent families are inventions of liberal divorce laws or of modern decades.

In modern America, many couples worry about the psychological effects of having children spaced too far apart. Some couples also worry about having only the number of children which they can afford to raise and educate. In the mid-nineteenth century, the joy of having another child far outweighed the jealousy it might cause in the psyche of any older siblings or any temporary financial difficulties it might create. Many families spanned generation lines, as women continued to have children as long as they were able. It was not unusual for children to have much older, and younger, siblings.

Elderly and single adults often lived with family members instead of keeping house for themselves. Among other chores, the relatives often helped with child care.

This family of nine people gathered outside for a group portrait, rather than in the confines of a photographer's studio.

4

The Nose Out of Joint
This lithograph, dealing with childhood jealousies, was printed in The Mother's Journal and Family Visitant *for September 1861. The magazine was published by Sheldon & Co. of New York.*

It was not unusual for children to have much older and much younger siblings.

To express it in accounting terms, children were assets, not liabilities, in a household, as they were given chores which enabled them to contribute to the family. In an agricultural society, an extra child was an extra farmhand. Boys were encouraged to work in the family business or farm, and girls were trained to help with domestic tasks. This benefitted the children, as well as the family: from an early age, children felt the self-worth which comes from having responsibilities.

Nepotism—giving family members preference in employment practices—was not only desirable, it was a rule of thumb. If employing relatives in the family business did not always bring people with natural skills to the jobs, it at least brought people with years of familiarity with the way things were done.

The ties of blood were long, and families which fell on hard times could often count on relatives to offer an opportunity or job. This is precisely the role which journal writer Judith McGuire's brother played in her life after she fled Richmond.

Society and Communities

A willingness to help out near or distant relatives shows the way in which most Americans viewed those who had fallen on hard times. In this land of opportunity, being poor was most often a temporary state. When help was offered to those in need, it very often included a job and any training that the individual or family would need to prosper.

Even with hard work, Americans recognized that a family that had been "making it" could be reduced to destitution by losing several years of crops, or losing a father, or seeing their just-filled barn burn to the ground. In a land without banking regulations, mortgage holders could evict at will, calling in debts at any time. Americans recognized that being poor was not so suspicious or tragic as staying poor.

This man wears the rough clothing of a teamster or other laborer. The backmark indicates that this photograph was taken in Camden, N.J.

Some Americans were desperately poor. This group generally included families without wage earners and those without housing. Fiction from the period often includes heartrending descriptions of mothers who freeze to death trying to warm their toddlers.

The wave of immigrants from Ireland and other European countries had already begun, and many of them arrived destitute. The earlier immigrants survived and prospered, but as the decades progressed, the numbers overwhelmed the opportunities available, and it became increasingly difficult for the later arrivals to find security.

Those who were permanently poor—or who appeared unwilling to work their way up—were viewed with pity. Pictorials of child beggars were particularly tragic, for they offered no hope that the individual was getting any help (including temporary support). In one children's book of the period, a wealthy child who decides to help a beggar child is encouraged not to give

This child was taken to the photographer's studio dressed up in a gown made of an extremely rough textured fabric. This child was probably from a family of modest means.

These three boys wear suits of clothing that are in the process of being "handed down." Each of the older boys wears a jacket that matches the pants worn by his younger brother. Once the jackets are passed down, each boy will be wearing a suit with jacket and pants that match.

This photograph was taken in St. Louis, Missouri. The boy wears an outfit which is elaborately trimmed. The rocking horse was a photographer's prop not a personal plaything.

her money, but instead to pray for her, offering a permanent, rather than temporary, solution to the problem.

America had a reputation for being a "land of opportunity" where just about anyone could get ample food and decent shelter, and someday own the means to his own livelihood. Those who achieved this goal formed the vast majority of Americans. By modern standards, they may not have had much property, but of the food/clothing/shelter necessities, they had enough for themselves, and often a bit left over which they could share with the less fortunate.

There were also, of course, those who had far more than they needed and this small portion of the population formed the elite. Most Americans acknowledged the community leaders who had a lot (or just a little) more than anyone else, but the actual wealth of these community leaders varied greatly. In a frontier community, it might be someone with a horse in addition to the more practical oxen. On Wall Street, that man would be a poor relation. A person's status in society was very much a function of the community in which he lived.

Most Americans lived in small, close-knit communities. Americans who lived in large cities generally existed in community-like neighborhoods. Even those who lived on isolated farms, far from their nearest neighbor, generally had some town or community center with which they maintained contact, and to which they traveled to purchase items they could not produce. Men in a community often had similar concerns for the issues of the day, whether of national, state, or the purely local interest.

Americans had not yet developed their modern preoccupation with organized and professional sports. They knew political platforms, rather than sports rosters. Men's social clubs, fire companies and fraternities were more often involved in religious or political discussions and demonstrations than in sports tournaments and competitions.

Lester Frank Ward, was a typical (if intellectual) young man. In 1861, he was attending the Institute at Towanda, Pennsylvania, and while a student there, he joined a debating society. The debate topics he noted in his journal show the topics and level of analysis given to issues of the day:

Resolved: that genius has more than circumstances to make great men.

Resolved: that war is a worse evil than slavery.

Question: will republics ultimately surpass all other governments?[3]

The sense of community gave individuals a sense of permanence and a sense of continuity. People not only knew their neighbors, they knew their neighbors' parents, and they expected to know each other for a long time to come.

Americans who lived in large cities generally existed in community-like neighborhoods. This is a photograph of Broadway, above Canal Street, in New York City.

Chapter II
Everyday Life In America

Occupations

The 1860 (eighth) Census pointedly stated that manufacturing in America had grown to such a size that it provided employment for one in every six working Americans. However, this was still an agrarian society, and more Americans were involved in growing crops and raising animals than any other occupation. Because of the climate or soil in a given area, farmers often raised the same crops as their neighbors. A great majority of the farmers were also the sons of farmers; men who had followed in the footsteps of their fathers. Farming required the sort of instinctive knowledge of "when to do what" that was learned through a lifetime of exposure to the occupation.

Like many Americans, debater Lester Frank Ward was the son of a farmer. Like a minority of Americans, he chose *not* to follow in the footsteps of his father. Instead, he initially trained to make wheel hubs, and then became, later in life, a school teacher, soldier, author, and college professor.

For the minority of men who did not follow in their fathers' footsteps, there were plenty of alternative occupations. Occupations of the period were sometimes divided into trades, (which taxed the body more than the mind), and professions, (which taxed the mind more than the body).

Men who wished to enter the trades—to be farriers, founders, drivers, or engineers—generally needed specialized training. A father who could not provide a son with that training could arrange for him to become an apprentice to a skilled craftsman. However, these arrangements were generally less formal than the indentures and apprenticeships of earlier eras. Nonetheless, they provided the young men with the benefit of training from someone skilled and experienced in the field, and with the use of the tools of the trade. At the end of such a training program, a young man might open his own business, or take over the clientele of an older craftsman who wished to see his business continue beyond his lifetime.

A man who posed for a photograph with a horse might have been the horse's owner. However, it is also possible he could be the horse's groom.

A man who posed for a picture with a saw was probably a carpenter. Notice his straw hat thrown on the floor behind the chair.

This minister posed with a prayer book for his photograph.

Men who wished to enter the professions—to become lawyers, ministers, professors, bankers, and representatives of the government—generally required money, education and/or social prominence. A father with money who wished to improve his son's social prominence might send him off to a prestigious school where he could form friendships with those who might help him find a position in society. However, in America, the land of opportunity, there were also self-made men, like Abraham Lincoln and Isaac Singer, who parlayed their tradesmen's upbringings into professions and prominence; Lincoln as a lawyer, and Singer as executive of a multi-national sewing machine company.

Like the rail-splitter Abraham Lincoln, and like the tool-and-dye maker Isaac Singer, hub-maker Lester Frank Ward was ambitious enough to go on to a professional career.

In a tone which will remind the modern reader of "if I were a rich man" Ward predicted what he would do with his first hundred dollars:

> If I had a hundred dollars I should buy a fine complete outfit, a good strong valise and several other indispensable things. Then I should go to New York, Niagara Falls and several other places.[4]

The man who sat for a portrait with his newspaper may have been the owner, or editor of the paper. Technology was so much prized in this period that the printer would more likely have posed with his press than with its product.

There is a legend about Abraham Lincoln that he walked several miles to return a few pennies change to a customer. In a society where barter was the norm, a few pennies cash was a significant amount. Like Lincoln, Ward kept careful count of pennies: he took watchful note of all progress toward his first hundred dollars:

> I left Thursday with my load of hubs....I argued with two wagon-makers and finally succeeded in trading twenty-five sets for a watch like my brother's....I stopped with another wagon-builder and gave him a set of hubs and twenty-five cents for my entertainment....I argued with the hardware dealer, bought three augers, two knives and a watch...I am very proud of my watch. From this lot I got 25 + 6 + 1-1/2 = 32-1/2 toward my hundred dollars.[5]

"Why should it be less creditable to make good dresses than bad books?" The sewing machine was one of the first consumer goods which could be purchased on "time." Ownership of sewing machines was fast becoming commonplace, but for many families, even the $5 per month payment was a struggle. The industrial revolution—and consumer goods like sewing machines—reached the south somewhat slower than the north, and so it is that this couple from Salem, North Carolina, are so proud of their sewing machine, that they've included it in their portrait.

The preceding discussion of trades and professions omits an important class of workers: women. While most worked in the home, there was a substantial minority with full- or part-time businesses. Professional women, and women craftsmen, were more common in the mid-nineteenth century than is generally believed. Many sources of information about the period mention only the socially respectable occupations which were closely related to domestic skills: governess, teacher, domestic servant. The trend of emphasizing and glorifying some, but not other feminine occupations was deplored even during the period. One contemporary author complained about "mothers, who would rather take for a daughter-in-law the poorest governess, the most penniless dependent, than a 'person in business'—milliner, dress-maker, shop-woman &c....Why should it be less creditable to make good dresses than bad books?"[6]

It had not always been so. In colonial times, and in frontier areas, the household was a unit of production. Men and women worked together on family farms, or pioneer settlements, equitably sharing tasks. Born of necessity and common sense, these self-sufficient arrangements produced the food and clothing, made repairs and improvements, offered security, and raised the children. Nearly everything needed for the family could be produced in-house (so to speak). Often, there was more than enough and the excess could be sold or traded for other products. In these production households, women were equal partners, and in this early period (1750-1815), women shared economic equality and political activism with men. Their value in the production household was obvious and unquestioned.

Throughout the first and second quarter of the nineteenth century, more and more commercially produced goods and services became available. As a result, the household (except in the most rural or remote areas), developed into a unit of consumption, rather than a unit of production. The woman of the household might sew clothes, but she did not weave fabric. She might raise chickens and keep a cow, but she went to the local market to purchase other foodstuffs. In the transition from producer to consumer, the perception of woman's worth suffered. She was still valued, but as a manager of the household and as a teacher of children, rather than as an equal partner who shared the husband's role of producing household income. There were, of course, some women who pursued professions and some who became just as successful as their male counterparts. However, for the vast majority, domestic life overshadowed any possibility of a professional career.

In an era which pre-dated the most basic labor-saving devices, virtually every household task was time-consuming and physically demanding. The effort and skill required was obvious. Almost all women had domestic help—in the form of children who performed chores, and female relatives who visited or lived in the same household.

As more and more men worked in large industrial complexes away from home, women and children had fewer opportunities to participate in the professions of their husbands. In wealthier families, this led to a much-studied phenomenon in which some women confined their activities entirely to the "domestic sphere."

Women of the more middling sort of families often did not have the luxury of restricting themselves to any one sphere of activity. Women (and children) in less affluent families took in laundry, sold butter and eggs or baked goods, and took their turn at plowing the family garden or running their own home-based businesses.

Some girls in the mid-nineteenth century did take jobs outside the family home, but it was generally an intermediate step between school and family. This was especially true of the "factory girls" hired in the textile mills of the northeast. In the 1820s and 1830s, mills (like the ones at Lowell, Massachusetts) which specialized in the employment of farm girls, were social and industrial pioneers. They encouraged respectable young girls from the surrounding farms to spend a few years working (and supplying the owners with a cheap, dependable labor force), then return to their communities to become wives and mothers. Employment records show that few stayed for very many years, and the accounts left by the girls themselves indicate that they considered their jobs to be temporary arrangements.

Lucy Larcom was such a girl. She started work in the mills at age 11 and later in life, published a book containing her remembrances of those years.

Country girls were naturally independent, and the feeling that at this new work the few hours they had of every-day leisure were entirely their own was a satisfaction to them. They preferred it to going out as "hired help." It was like a young man's pleasure in entering upon business for himself. Girls had never tried that experiment before, and they liked it. It brought out in them a dormant strength of character which the world did not previously see, but now fully acknowledges. Of course they had a right to continue at that freer kind of work as long as they chose, although their doing so increased the perplexities of the housekeeping problem for themselves even, since many of them were to become, and did become, American house-mistresses.[7]

Eventually, the mill owners discovered an even cheaper labor force in immigrants, and the character of the grand experiment changed.

The photograph of Miss Ella Owen was taken in Lowell, Massachusetts. She is the same age as many "mill girls" and appears uncomfortable with the ribbon that she or someone else purchased for her dress.

Marriage

Most men and women expected to marry some day. Men considered it very much preferable to be king of their own castles than to board or live with relatives. Women also considered marriage preferable to "living in" as a maiden aunt. These maiden aunts often "boarded around" earning their keep by cooking, sewing or watching young children in siblings' households. Autograph books of the period are filled with sentiments like: "A long life and a good husband is the sincere wish of your friend."[8]

Finding a mate was the goal of many a young man and woman in the mid-nineteenth century. Those who found a potential mate courted under the watchful eye of their families and their communities.

Lester Frank Ward was no exception, and he was deeply in love.

I have written a little to the sweet girl, whose daguerreotype I have. How I love her, and how I want to kiss her! We shall be married, my sweetness, some day, never fear....

My darling, I am going to read this with you within my arm, and kiss you ten times at the same time. Kiss my picture, if not my letters....[9]

Although public manners required that Americans restrain displays of passion, private manners between lovers (married, as well as unmarried) were quite different, and may have been all the more enjoyable for the secrecy.

It is a further indication of the importance of family that engagements were considered very serious business, and were considered to be legally binding. There are still laws which allow parties to sue each other for breaking an engagement, but they are little-known and seldom

This couple posed for a wedding portrait dressed in their wedding clothes. The groom wears a frock coat with light colored pants and vest, while the bride wears a white day dress and veil.

This bride posed alone for a portrait, wearing the white day dress which served as her wedding gown. The dress itself has long sleeves and a relatively close-fitted neckline befitting modest brides. Her veil is floor-length, and, like others of this period, appears to be made of net.

This may be a photograph of an entire wedding party, or it may be a photograph taken to celebrate an engagement. Note, first, that the seated couple are holding hands, a very unusual pose for this period. The three women appear to be dressed identically, and it was commonplace for the bridesmaids and the bride to dress alike. (Thus many photographs of a bride and groom with the maid of honor and best man have been mis-identified as "double wedding" photographs.)

invoked. By contrast, in the mid-nineteenth century, these laws were common knowledge. Books of "useful household information" included information on enforcing them.

> 2047 BREACH OF PROMISE OF MARRIAGE—...A verbal offer of marriage is sufficient whereon to ground an action for breach of promise of marriage. The conduct of the suitor, subsequent to the breaking off the engagement, would weigh with the jury in estimating damages....[10]

As in most other eras, weddings of the mid-nineteenth century varied greatly. Couples with time, money, and inclination might have large, formal festivities, while others simply visited a local clergyman with (or without) members of their immediate family.

Young couples (generally) looked forward to raising large families. Infants were welcomed with love, affection, and—relief. Mortality rates for women in childbirth and newborn infants were extremely high, and any birth without a death was a cause for celebration. Indeed, death in childbirth was so common that pregnant women typically made arrangements for the foster care of their children, should they die while in labor. There was at least one incident in which a pregnant woman became so confident of her impending death in childbirth that she specified the box she was to be buried in afterwards.[11]

Infants and Mortality

The love of babies was basic to Americans. Few worse things could be said about an individual, than that he or she did not love an infant. It is a point which Virginian Anne S. Frobel makes in her diary when speaking of a (northern) boarder at her home:

> Thursday, Nov. 6, 1862 ...Among other horrible things she told was the death of her only child, a little infant, she said she was glad it was dead, she did not want the trouble of it, she had no feeling, or care of love for it whatever. To be sure when she saw it in its death struggle it lifted its little arm and seemed to be in such agony she did feel a little sorry for it, but she was glad it was dead, and all her trouble with it was over, and then she laughed. I listened to the woman's talk until I was sick and disgusted.[12]

Few worse things could be said about an individual than that he or she did not love an infant.

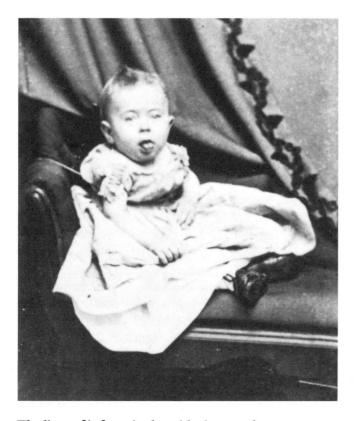

The lives of infants in the mid-nineteenth century were not entirely different from those of modern babies.

The lives of infants in the mid-nineteenth century were not entirely different from that of modern babies: They ate, slept, cried, and were cuddled and fed. However, this was an era before the invention of disposable diapers, and even rubber pants. Infants were dressed in cloth "napkins"—as many as five at a time.

In all but the wealthiest households, babies were generally kept in the kitchen during the day. There were several practical reasons for this: first, most houses did not have central heat, and the kitchen was the warmest room in the house. Second, women spent much of their time in and around the kitchen, and they could save time and steps by having the baby close at hand.

Mothers looking for advice on taking care of their babies very often had the advantage of more experienced female relatives who lived with the family, or would stay to help out in the first weeks or months. At least one "Grandmama" had published a book of advice on taking care of children, and she included instructions on every conceivable topic, from sitting a basin in one's lap when holding an infant, to constructing infant clothes with tie fasteners.

Another thing in the dress of infants...deserves also to be imitated; which is, that not one pin is employed in their clothing, every article that requires to be fastened, having strings....[13]

Pins were the least of the worries for many mothers. An infant's health was a constant concern. If a baby took ill, mothers had to choose between their own home remedies—and their own instincts on dosage; or patent medicines—and risk uneven batches, and impurities. Commercial medicines were prepared and sold without government regulation, and often contained ingredients now known to be harmful and/or addictive. Laudanum, for example (an opium derivative), is a highly addictive drug which was commonly sold for the relief of teething pain.

Throughout the nation, but especially in rural areas, much of the medical care administered in the mid-nineteenth century was based on folk medicine. Every large family or community included someone with a reputation for knowing what to do for the sick or injured. That person might—or might not—have had formal training. There were, however, times when a problem was beyond the scope of local knowledge and abilities. Sometimes, in spite (or because) of the best care available, infants and children took ill and died.

The death of an infant was a great tragedy, but Americans comforted themselves by preserving the

Infant gowns were much longer than the children themselves. The long skirts helped to keep the babies covered even when they squirmed around in bed. As they got older, the children's gowns were shortened (like the one on the right), which allowed them to learn to walk.

memory of the child, and looking forward to a reunion in the next life. In an era when waste was considered a great sin, every garment, every toy, associated with a dead child was passed on to the next child. Parents who wanted a special remembrance of the dead child very often had its photograph taken after death. Many of these post-mortem photographs, taken and cherished as mementoes of love to those who had "gone before," still exist today as reminders of this practice.

The habit of preserving a lock of hair from a loved one is another practice of this same sentiment. In the military, soldiers sometimes cut a lock of hair from a fallen comrade, and sent or took it home for the wife or family of the fallen one.

Locks of hair were also cut from the heads of famous individuals, and in the 1870s, when Robert E. Lee died, his personal physician, Dr. Barton cut a lock from his

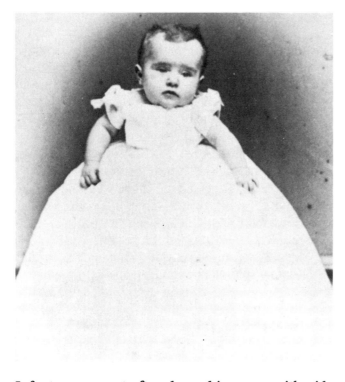

Infants were most often dressed in gowns with wide necklines, short sleeves, and voluminous skirts.

head and preserved it. Far from the souvenir-hunting which is seen when modern fans seek to collect garments from music stars, this was an act of reverence. Indeed, late in his life, Dr. Barton wrote a letter apologizing to his children that he had "nothing of value" to bequeath them. Yet they inherited an envelope of Lee's hair.

To modern Americans, post-mortem photographs, and locks of disembodied hair may seem "morbid" and "unpleasant." Understanding and appreciating that these were loving reminders of family members requires an understanding of the nineteenth century attitude toward death: Death is so much a taboo topic in modern society, that it is easiest to discuss the topic through analogy. The contrast between mid-nineteenth century and modern attitudes toward death can be better understood by comparing it with attitudes toward sex in those same periods.

In modern American culture, death is a taboo topic: The death of an individual is not a topic for general discussion, and in polite conversation, death is generally referred to with euphemisms (such as "passed away"). Individuals who have experienced the death of a loved one are encouraged to grieve, but to swiftly "get over" the incident, and "get on" with life. While it is acknowledged that everyone will someday encounter the death of a friend or family member, little emphasis is placed on preparing children for death before it is necessary to do so. The open discussion of death is considered unpleasant, at best.

In modern American society, the reverse is true of sex. Not only is it discussed in public, but it is a favorite theme in novels and other forms of entertainment. The open discussion of sex, even with young children, is considered healthy, perhaps even a necessity.

In the mid-nineteenth century, attitudes toward these two topics were reversed. Sex in the mid-nineteenth century (like death today) was a taboo topic seldom discussed in polite society. Expressions of sexual love were kept as private as grieving is today.[14]

Death, on the other hand, was openly and honestly discussed. It formed an important theme in many novels and other forms of entertainment. Death and the afterlife were discussed with extremely young children, even before a beloved friend or pet died.

The open discussion of death did not belittle it, and Americans were never completely prepared for the death of a family member, particularly a child or infant. Generally, medical care was administered at home, and parents could find comfort in gently caring for a child in its last hours, then grieving together at the loss.

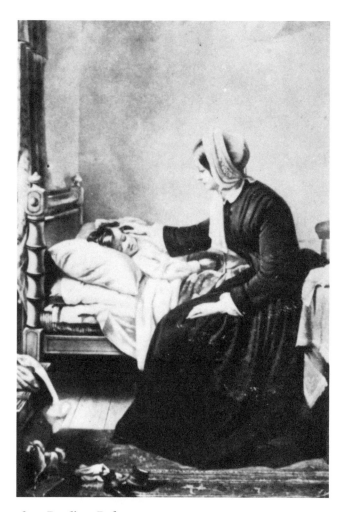

Our Darling Babe

'Twas hard to part with our dear babe,
But, oh! how sweet to feel
That God, who gave, who took away,
Can all our sorrows heal;
He sent the gem to win our hearts
From pleasures here below,
To fit us for the coming day
When we are called to go.

She is a little angel now,
And wears a crown of gold:
With outstretched arms she beckons us
To keep within his fold:
She says "Come mother, father, dear,
For unto all 'tis given
To meet, to join, to part no more
At his bright throne in heaven."

Excerpt from a Civil War period album compiled near Hollidaysburg, Pennsylvania.

Few things could express the loss of a child as well as the look on this grieving father's face.

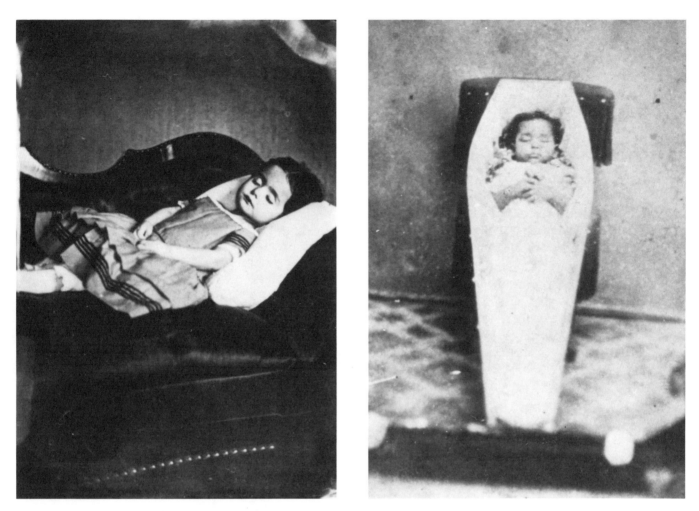

When post-mortem or after-death photographs were taken, the individuals were often laid out in a natural position, and made to appear as though they were merely sleeping. The photograph of a child taken in a coffin is less common than those taken in more life-like poses. Many photographers advertised that they would make house-calls to take post-mortem photographs. Thus the families did not have to carry the corpse to the photographer's studio.

A Family Mourns

This photograph shows a woman holding a child in her lap, with another at her side. All are dressed in black, and the woman appears to have a crepe covering over her dress. It is unusual for children in mourning to be dressed in black; they were more traditionally dressed in white with black trim for mourning. However, the conviction that she holds a dead (rather than sleeping) child in her lap is supported by the evidence that she holds it by a single leg, which would seem an unusually casual way to hold a child. It may be that the child is merely sleeping, and that the entire family is dressed in deep mourning for another.

Children and Education

These children posed for their picture holding toys which were probably homemade playthings: balls of tightly wound scrap fabric.

Parents watched over their infants with care, and rejoiced when a sickly infant showed signs of survival through the early period of life. A child's first step was a special event in part because it was simply a sign of good health. As infants grew into toddlers and became mobile, they were dressed in short, knee-length gowns that they might not trip on their clothing. Boys and girls alike were dressed in gowns and skirts, which permitted easy access to napkins (diapers) needing to be changed.

Toddlers and young children spent much of their time in the kitchen, and in the yard between the house and the garden. In and around the kitchen, they found wooden spoons, corn cobs, and other indestructible household implements to use as playthings. In most households, most playthings were homemade. The prevalence of homemade and make-do toys is often overlooked because visual information often conflicts with the concept: Lithographs often show doting parents giving their children manufactured toys, on occasions like Christmas or a birthday, and children frequently posed for photographs holding toy props used by the photographer for numerous portraits.

Children used their imagination to play with items intended for some other purpose. There is little evidence that they suffered due to the lack of numerous manufactured toys. Indeed, a pet dog or cat in a modern American household frequently has more manufactured toys than children of the mid-nineteenth century.

At an early age, children were given their first chores, and their first responsibilities. Boys were encouraged to take care of animals, work outside, or spend time in their father's shop, while girls were taught household chores.

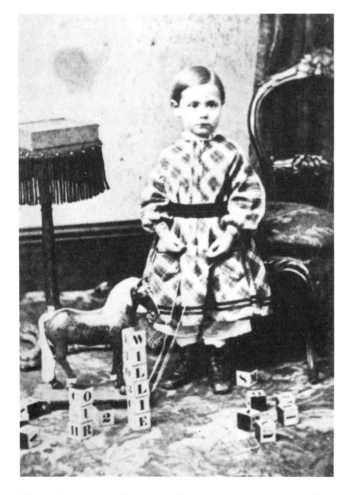

This photograph is as much a photo of the toys as it is of the boy. The blocks tell us that "Our Willie" is 2.

At an early age, children were given their first chores, and their first responsibilities. It is curious, though, that this child was photographed while dressed up to do chores.

From chair moving, bed making, and floor waxing, we went up gradually to setting the table, keeping the knives, forks and spoons bright, washing and drying the dishes, and "above all else in importance" was the keeping of everything in its appointed place, for everything had its place. Knitting and sewing came in due time...We learned to beat the eggs and cream the butter and mix all after the proper and careful preparation by helping to do it; and in the same way we learned to dress a chicken or turkey, to try out the lard, to make souse and sausage and soap....[15]

When family finances required it, children were sometimes expected to hire out and contribute their earnings to the family income. Nineteenth century literature is filled with accounts of children and young teens who were required to leave school and go to work during hard times. Miss Catherine Lawrence, related this story of her own life:

...Within 3 months I lost my father and mother. I had just reached the age of fourteen and was left homeless. I had acquired a thorough knowledge of the common English branches and had commenced in several of the higher studies, but now the time had come for me to leave school. I must earn my living.[16]

Catherine Lawrence continued her education on her own, and eventually became a school teacher, public speaker and activist in the cause of abolition.

School was an important topic in the lives of most children. Few states provided universal public education, but in communities throughout the nation, local church congregations and civic-minded citizens started schools. The teacher was often left largely to his or her own devices, and the day-to-day running of the schools was based more on the teacher's practices than the board's policies. The agricultural economy dictated school schedules, and children were excused from school during the months when they were needed in the fields. The modern practice of closing schools for long summer breaks is an archaic holdover of this practice.

Has this child has been doing some chore which has colored her hands up to her wrist?

Little girls were expected to become accomplished seamstresses, and to take up some sort of decorative needlework, as time permitted. This girl appears to be doing needlepoint on a canvas backing. Notice the work basket on the table beside her.

These young girls are just old enough to be reading and reciting their lessons. Often, children started out by memorizing the scriptures they heard in church, and reciting them at home.

The schools were generally small, and often several grade levels were taught in the same room. Testing was often oral, and children memorized and recited more often than they wrote. Indeed, there is some evidence that the phrase "toeing the line" relates to the practice of making children stand at a line on the floor when reciting their lessons. In order to focus on their own lessons when others were reciting, children developed skills in concentration to rival the modern student who can listen to loud music and do homework at the same time.

Corporal punishment was used, and even encouraged. Lucy Chase traveled south to teach in a school for free blacks. She related in a letter that the mothers frequently encouraged her to use corporal punishment:

Norfolk, VA 7/1/64

...Many a father and mother have begged me to beat their children at school. "Spare the rod and spoil the child," is on every mothers tongue. "Now you whip her and make a good girl out of her," the kindest mother says when she trusts her sweetest child to us....[17]

In small communities, it was not unusual for children to be taught by young women who were sisters, cousins, or otherwise related to the students in the class. A student who excelled in his or her own studies was often asked to help out by teaching others. This family portrait seems to show one who would not "take her nose out of the book," even to sit for a family portrait.

In general, students attended school for fewer years than do modern students. However, a brief survey of school books from the period indicates that their reading books advanced through several modern grade levels in any given year. By the fifth year of school, students were reading material at a level which is today considered college level.[18]

There were also academies, which provided intensive educational experiences. The children of wealthy families might board at the academy, while children from the area were day students. These academies offered a variety of classes. John B. Cary's Hampton (VA.) Male and Female Academy, for example, offered classes in Greek, Latin, French, German, Italian and Spanish, as well as chemistry, natural philosophy and astronomy. As at most academies, the boys and girls were kept separated at Hampton.

At many southern academies, discipline was maintained among the boys through a military-type training which well prepared them for military service. It not only prepared the students, but also the faculty. Indeed, John B. Cary's academy closed during the war, as 20% of the faculty, and 25% of the students served together in a unit which became the 32nd Virginia Infantry.

A family sending a child to an academy was paying tuition and, often, boarding fees. In addition the family was doing without any income that the child might have made at a part-time job. Thus students who boarded at and attended schools like Cary's Hampton academy were the exception, rather than the rule.

Many teens were expected to contribute to the welfare of the family, and to continue doing so until they had a family of their own. Most Americans did not marry for the first time until they were in their twenties, and with children who began working (at least part-time) in their early teens, families could count on nearly a decade of time during which their children contributed to the family resources.

The Westtown Boarding School, Chester Co., Pa., opened in 1799. These female students were photographed in 1864 by John Moran.

Growing Up

As in more modern eras, teens sought to assert their independence and to differentiate themselves from children by, among other things, changing their styles of fashion and hair. Boys began wearing vests and hats, and as their feet stopped growing, many got their first pair of boots. Teenage girls lengthened their dresses from mid-calf to ankle, and even to the floor. They grew their hair longer, and often wore it in the hair nets so popular during the middle decades of the nineteenth century.

One of the more subtle differences between child and adult clothing for females was the location of the fasteners. Girls, who had help with their toilettes, often had dresses and bodices which fastened at the center back. Adult women, who dressed without assistance, most often had bodices which fastened at the center front.

For young American girls, the transition from back-to front-fastening bodices was a symbol of growing up. When she was sixteen, Caroline Cowles Richards wrote in her journal:

> I wanted my dress waist which Miss Rosewarne is making to hook up in the front, but Grandmama said I would have to wear it that way all the rest of my life so I had better be content to hook it in the back a little longer....It is nice, though, to dress in style and look like other people. I have a Garibaldi waist and a Zouave jacket and a balmoral skirt.[19]

Another characteristic of teens at the time which is still noticeable today was their inclination to adopt fads faster than their older contemporaries. As with children today, teens of the mid-nineteenth century sometimes picked up information in school about the "latest things." For example, Carolyn Cowles Richards tells in her diary of receiving instructions in gymnastics while attending the academy in her home town.[20]

To those who believe that a preoccupation with health and physical fitness is a recent phenomenon, gymnastics might seem a surprising addition to mid-nineteenth century curriculum.

In her braid-decorated Garibaldi blouse this young lady is wearing "the latest fashion" for the mid-years of the war. The shirt was styled—and named—after the flamboyant uniform of the Italian patriot, Giuseppe Garibaldi. The shirt style remained popular through the end of the Civil War.

Unlike the young lady in her Garibaldi shirt, this girl wears a dress with the characteristics of a child's dress. It has the wide neckline and short sleeves seen more often in children's clothing. In addition, it opens at the back.

These two photographs show individuals wearing loose, comfortable clothing recommended in gymnastic exercise manuals of the period. Men were encouraged to have their shirts button to the pants (in the manner of small boys), so that they would not need to wear braces (or suspenders) when exercising. Women were encouraged to remove their hoops and corsets, and wear outfits with loose bodices, relatively short skirts, and trousers. This outfit was very much like the bathing dress of the day. However, the exercise manuals also stated that individuals could exercise in their street dress, provided the men removed their coats, and the women removed their hoops.
The photographs also show typical gymnastic equipment of the day: dumbbells, rings, and wands. An important part of the exercise program was the recitation of poetry or songs, which helped the participants to keep time. Some gymnastic manuals included sheet music written for the various exercises.

Exercise classes were offered in schools, and at public gymnasiums in many towns. Public classes were very often "mixed," allowing men and women to exercise together, which may surprise those with pre-conceived notions about "Victorian" sensibilities.

The emphasis of health and fitness programs was not on beauty. Men of the mid-nineteenth century admired an ideal beauty who had a round, moon face with pale ivory complexion. Her plump hands belied small wrists, and her wide hips emphasized her small waist. It was not an ideal that would be achieved through exercise. As in many eras, fashion dictated the ideal, mortals simply did the best they could.

The delicate woman who was considered an ideal beauty might be admired, and courted, but men were encouraged to marry healthy women, and (more importantly) women with the skills and talents in housekeeping. This attitude (which has not entirely disappeared), is reflected in phrases like "the way to a man's heart is through his stomach," or (in the elegant phrasing of the time):

You may be as beautiful as Venus and as talented as Madame de Stael, but you'll never reign supreme in your liege lord's affections, till you can roast a turkey.[21]

Relationships between men and women also followed different guidlines in the 19th century. For example, the group of potential mates was somewhat smaller than for the modern Americans who might meet thousands of other teens through school and sports activities. However, the universe was not as small as it might otherwise seem, since having similar ages was relatively unimportant. Indeed, it was relatively common, and generally acceptable, for girls in their twenties to marry men in their forties and even fifties.

Generally, courting was a family affair. The interested parties had plenty of siblings to watch and listen, but in addition to this, much of the entertainment of the day involved the entire family. While there were occasional parties, often held at the close of a community-effort event such as a corn-shucking, these were the exception rather than the rule. Most evenings were spent in a parlor or kitchen with the rest of the family and any others who had gathered. Everyone was expected to take part in an evening's entertainment, from the youngest toddler capable of reciting a rhyme to the suitor who could (or could not) sing for his intended. When there was a party or gathering that included a number of single young adults, group activities often included games like "forfeits" (which involved challenges and penalties), "blind man's bluff," and kissing games.

This engraving of "Fall Games—The Apple Bee" appeared in Harper's Weekly. It depicts the sort of group activity enjoyed by young men and women.

The Civil War period occurred at a time in history when men publicly expressed emotions like affection and grief without being thought weak. Expressions of romantic love were not so public, and the evidence of some romances is found only through the existence of private letters, Valentines, and "sentimentals" like this bank note. A pencilled comment on the note indicates it may have been exchanged with a proposal of marriage.

Chapter III
Civilian Influences on the Military

T hose who wish to understand the actions and experiences of Civil War soldiers must understand civilians of the mid-nineteenth century. One major reason for this is that more than 99% percent of the men who fought in the war had been civilians before they were tapped for service during the war. One such man was hub maker/debater Lester Frank Ward.

On the day that he decided to enlist and fight in the Civil War, Ward wrote a lengthy entry in his diary:

August 13, 1862

...Monday evening I got hold of John's horse and carriage and came back here to take my girl up to the mountain to pick berries Tuesday morning. Finding no one to accompany us, we set out alone...one of the wheels broke, and I had to go back to the city....After an hour and a half, I was once more ready to set out. We arrived on top of the mountain about noon. Consequently we were obliged to spend the night on the mountain. We had a sweet time.

Wednesday morning our horse got loose....What a condition! Alone on the mountain without a horse. Despair...at first.

I looked all day without finding him. Finally I persuaded a man to take us in the back of his wagon to the foot of the mountain, where I engaged a horse to bring us here again....Thursday... before we came back I broke the pole of the carriage. Friday morning...back to the mountain and find the horse. I found him.

This, it would seem, is the diary of a civilian, and not a man about to become a soldier. However, Ward wrote one last sentence in his journal entry:

This photograph shows a man in civilian dress, holding a military-style cap. He may be a civilian contemplating enlistment, or a former soldier who has returned to civilian life. There are many photographs of former soldiers who continued to wear military-style vests or other pieces of clothing after they left the military.

This remarkable pair of photographs are identified as Edward C. Bear. They seem to show a man, dressed and posed as a civilian surveyor, and then again, dressed and equipped as a surveyor for the military.

Saturday I spent the day learning about the war. I determined to enroll and thus finish this week full of events.[22]

Enlist he did, pausing just long enough to marry his girl. Nearly nine months to the day later, Ward lay on a hospital bed, writing a letter. It is the same articulate man:

Most worthy Friend
    Upon the bed of a wounded soldier might your humble servant be found this morning, endeavoring...to write...[a] synopsis of the great drama, as far as could be surveyed from the ranks of an obscure Regiment like our gallant 141st. ...I was chuckling over [the] grand opportunity offered me for thinning out the enemies of human liberty, when a silent messenger came, and entering the upper part of my right knee, glanced on the bone, and making its egress, passed to the rear, bringing me to the ground...a couple more of their friendly peacemakers came whizzing along in quick succession, making a pair of holes through me, in a workmanlike manner. The first...entered my left pants pocket and demolished a small wooden screw inkstand, passed through the thick muscle of my thigh, just missing the bone. The next one paid a similar tribute to the other thigh....[23]

Like thousands of other citizen-soldiers, Lester Frank Ward was an American who interrupted his otherwise civilian life to serve as a soldier in the war. Ward survived the war, but it left a permanent impression on his life as the leg wounds would bother him for the rest of his life.

While some men of military age hesitated to join up, others who were too young longed to go off with the others. This boy wears a military style cap and coat, but appears too young to be a soldier.

Individuals and the Military

The understanding that soldiers were themselves civilians leads to a better understanding of the ways in which their civilian culture—and personal ethics—are reflected in their military lives.

Just as Ward's pre-war personality is reflected in his wartime letters, so the basic culture of the mid-nineteenth century is reflected in the military processes and procedures, and in the actions and reactions of soldiers. The American frame of mind and individual ethics are revealed in the experiences of Civil War soldiers.

The soldier's code of ethics—like that of other Americans—was non-situational. Take, for example, a "found money" situation. If there is no possibility that the loser will miss it, and you need it (for a good cause) more than the loser, what is your responsibility to return "found" money? Today, incidents in which "found" money is returned are newsworthy. The general ethic seems to be that right is right only if it achieves some good end, and that wrong is okay if it doesn't harm anyone (and it might help you).

A Vermont soldier found himself in this precise situation when he discovered that the paymaster had paid him ten dollars more than his due. (This amount represented just about an extra month's salary, a sizeable windfall.) His reaction was not only to follow his code of ethics, but to see the incident as an example of God and Satan directly intervening in his life.

The interior of this church has been photographed decorated with garlands. Soldiers who were encamped in the same place for a period of time sometimes built permanent church structures. Others reported in their diaries that they helped to decorate the churches in communities where they camped.

Private Charlie Osgood lost one eye in battle, and developed myopia in the other eye. It is for this reason, perhaps, that he saved with his cherished letters and military papers, the Lord's Prayer, which he had inscribed in the size of a dime.

"And what are you going to do with it, Jim?"

"I confess that when bringing it to the tent I intended to keep it, and send it home. But God has preserved me from this great sin....The parting prayer of my mother was that I might not prove a coward, or become a drunkard. But she never dreamed that her son could become a thief....There, Mr. Satan, catch me asleep again if you can; you have got not only me to fight, but a good mother at home."[24]

In modern times, returning the money might be publicized as a good deed. This soldier asked his friends to keep mum, as he was ashamed that he had even carried the money back to his tent. The soldier clearly knew what was right. His hesitation was in acting on his principles.

In some cases, American military procedures were based on the conviction that soldiers would act on the principles they had learned as civilians. For example, there was the military practice of paroling prisoners of war: Taking prisoners of war is a well established military procedure. Prisoners are kept, reducing the enemy's forces, until the prisoners taken by each side are exchanged. However, it requires resources to guard and maintain the soldiers. It was not always possible to guard, keep and care for them. Relying on the conviction that a man's word was his bond, Civil War prisoners were sometimes "paroled." The prisoners swore they would not fight until officially exchanged, and were then released. It is a process which was followed throughout the war, and while the occasional soldier violated his parole, most could be trusted to stay out of the fight until exchanged.

Talk of ethics and religious principles naturally leads one to wonder how men so schooled in right and wrong could be induced to commit mass, repeated murder on the field of battle. At least for some, it was not in spite, but precisely because, of a sense of duty, that they fought:

Home is sweet and friends are dear, but what would they all be to let the country go to ruin, and be a slave. I am contented with my lot, in one sense of the word, for I know that I am doing my duty, and I know that it is my duty to do as I am now a-doing. If I live to get back, I shall be proud of the freedom I shall have, and know that I helped to gain that freedom. If I should not get back, it will do them good that do get back.[25]

The theme of home and family is a recurring one. Many of the soldiers were away from home for the first time, and the "family" was a primary concern and interest to the soldiers.

The steamer **New York** *returning paroled prisoners to be released behind their own lines. The prisoners swore they would not fight until officially exchanged, and were then released.*

Families and the Military

Men had been taught from an early age that their first duty was to God, family, and country. During the war, duty to God and country often conflicted with duty to God and family. The soldier faced a moral dilemma. When otherwise dedicated soldiers deserted—or thought about deserting—the army, it was often to return to their families in need. Others, especially those whose families were not endangered by the war, seemed to enjoy their time away, and expressed little regret at anything other than the inconvenience of being away from home.

In some cases, the pain of separation became too great to endure, and soldiers did desert the army. Mary Boykin Chesnut related such a story in her diary of society life in Richmond:

In 1861, battle seemed glamorous and exciting, and patriotic props were often used in studio photography. This young drummer appears as though he has seen the horrors of war.

The photograph is posed, but the sentiment is genuine. Many families received tragic news in letters written from the commanding officers or comrades of fallen soldiers. Others received more hopeful missives penned from hospital beds. Bad (and good) news was most often conveyed by letter: Telegraph lines were reserved for public, not private, messages.

Mothers sometimes dressed their young boys in clothing like their father's uniforms. These pictures were cherished reminders to the soldiers of the ones they left behind.

I was telling them today of a woman who came to Mrs. (Jefferson) Davis in Richmond, hoping to get her help. She wanted her husband's pardon. He was a deserter. The woman was shabbily dressed, chalk-white and with a pinched face. ...Her poor little Susie had just died, and the boy was ailing; food was so scarce and so bad. They all had chills, and she was so miserable. There was nobody to cut wood, and it was so cold. "The army was coming so near. I wrote, and I wrote: "If you want to see the baby alive, come! If they won't let you, come anyhow!" So you see, if he is a deserter, I did it. For they would not let him come. Only colonels and generals can get furloughs now. He only intended to stay one day, but we coaxed and begged him, and then he stayed and stayed; and he was afraid to go back afterwards....[26]

Soldiers heard their loved ones calling them, and yet most stayed in the military, continuing the fight, even when they wanted desperately to go home.

The decision to stay in the military was often made with misgivings. John French White was a native of Tidewater, Virginia. Early in the war, White and his comrades were ordered to abandon the peninsula of Virginia, leaving their homes and families behind Union lines. White worried constantly about the safety of his young family.

11/20/62

Dear Mat I must tell you I am in a hard place and know not what to do. When I think...how much my services are needed home I am temted to try and get there. I see no probability of getting there. ...How better can I die than defending my family and fireside. To do this I came in the war and now that you are threated I consider it my Christian duty to come to your rescue and protection. Dear Mat you know that I love my Country but I love my family better.[27]

Parthenia Antoinette Hague echoed the moral dilemma between duty to country and duty to family. Hague spent the war years living in Alabama, and after the war, published a memoir in which she described daily life during those hard times. "...[W]e, too, loved the Union our great and good Washington bequeathed us... but...'A man's family is the nearest piece of his country, and the dearest one.'"[28]

Children, who have very little sense of time, had difficulty understanding that brothers and fathers who stayed away for weeks and months at a time were EVER coming back. They also sensed the stress and fears felt by other family members, and for tens of thousands of children and their families, the fears were entirely justified.

Society and Communities in the Military

As the war broke out, neither the United States nor the Confederate States governments were fully equipped to organize and equip the large forces required for a major conflict. Indeed, some of the individual states were better equipped than the national governments. It seemed only natural that the class of civilian leaders should step in to help out. Wealthy or prominent men

This photograph shows Henry Brown and his wife, of Minneapolis, Minnesota. Like his brothers, Ed and Anson, Henry stopped to have his photograph taken before going to war. This photograph was made in Aurora, Illinois. The photographs of the three brothers, made in such different places, were brought together in a family album.

raised regiments, recruited the troops and financed their supplies of uniforms, equipment, and even arms. Often, these men were rewarded for their efforts by being given command of the troops they raised.

Not everyone agreed with this practice, especially when it was abused.

> So grand a nation must not—cannot—perish....[T]he brave men of the nation rushed to the rescue....But every selfish man, every politician, every trickster and trifler, saw a chance to "make a spec" out of it, and every Governor of a State and every secretary was besieged night and day for a commission:—"my son," or "nephew," or "a particular friend of mine," "must be looked after." No matter for the old country!—no matter for the flag!—no matter for the sanctified souvenirs

Ed and Anson Brown stopped off in Albany, New York, to have their photograph made as they left to go to war.

Everyone got into the act: These young men appear to be playing "Army," with one acting the part of a soldier (complete with carpetbag backpack), another barking orders (and holding a "sword" aloft), and two others (seated at the center) avoiding the draft entirely.

of our origin, nor the holy dead of the olden time. My son, or nephew, or friend, "must have a commission."

What came of all this? Whole cohorts, rank and file, from sheer thoughtlessness, the brave men of the nation were led to indiscriminate slaughter by incompetent officers![29]

Providing commissions to those who raised regiments was an accepted practice at the time of the Civil War. If it did not always ensure that officers would perform well under battle, it did attract men who were familiar with many of the less glamorous duties of an officer. Indeed, many of the administrative and managerial skills required of officers were precisely the skills needed for raising a regiment.

If the officers were ineffective leaders, there was a safety mechanism. When regiments were reorganized, soldiers elected their officers, and they could (and frequently did) vote down members of the privileged class who had shown themselves to be cowards—or martinets. In these cases, they often elected ordinary men like themselves who had demonstrated bravery and skill in combat. In the end, officers had to earn the respect, and admiration, of their soldiers.

One who earned that respect was Charles Fisher. Fisher had begun his career managing his family's agricultural enterprises, and then had risen in political prominence and was made president of the North Carolina Railroad. At the call for troops, he resigned his position with the Railroad to create a regiment. Many of his railroad workers followed him into the army. They, with Fisher as Colonel, were destined to be valuable troops, for their skills in repairing trains were greatly needed in the army.

Fisher must have found his duties managing the troops little different than they had been when working for the railroad. As president of the Railroad, he himself wrote a personal letter of sympathy when one of his workers was killed in a railroad accident. He even penned a note to arrange for transportation of the body. The man had worked for his railroad for only a few months. Yet it was Fisher—and not a subordinate—who penned the note. How many times would he repeat this

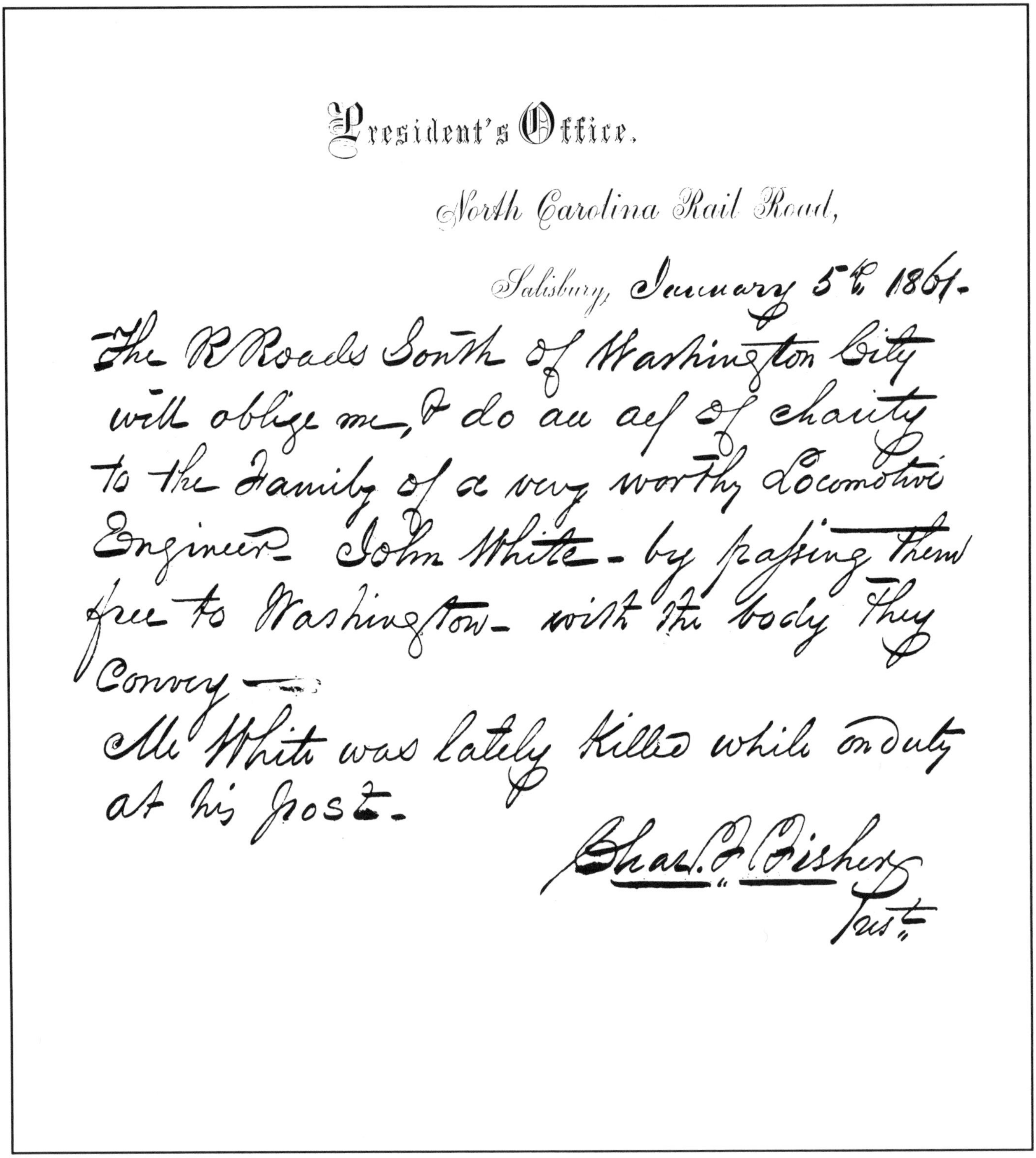

North Carolina Rail Road,

Salisbury, January 5ᵗʰ 1861.

The R Roads South of Washington City will oblige me, & do an act of charity to the Family of a very worthy Locomotive Engineer—John White—by passing them free to Washington with the body they convey.

Mr. White was lately killed while on duty at his post.

Chas. F. Fisher
Pest.

January 5, 1861

    The R Roads South of Washington City will oblige me, & do an act of charity to the Family of a very worthy Locomotive Engineer—John White—by passing them free to Washington with the body they convey.
    Mr. White was lately killed while on duty at his post.
Charles F. Fisher
President

grim task as his men worked in an even more dangerous industry? How many times would he, or his subordinates, have to arrange for the transportation of bodies being sent home?[30]

As it turned out, Colonel Fisher was killed in his first charge, in his first engagement, at the Battle of First Manassas. It was not he, but others, who arranged for the transportation of the bodies.

In many ways, the structure of Civil War military organizations reflected the structure of society: Companies of soldiers represented communities of citizens, and the officers represented the elite of society.

Letter of sympathy written by Charles Fisher to Mrs. White:

I write to you to express what we all feel most deeply, my [sincere] sympathy in your great affliction and bereavement.

Your husband has been on the Road only a few months, but this was long enough to gain him the respect and good will of us all. He had my confidence and regard as a most worthy excellent and reliable man—faithful in duty and unexceptionably exemplary in conduct.

It has pleased Almighty God to make you the chief sufferer under a most mysterious and terrible dispensation....
[the letter continues on another page and is signed]
Charles Fisher

Chapter IV
Civilian Participation In The War

Soldiers

Military units were generally community-based and (with the exception of "regular" army units), state-designated. Often, communities provided the manpower for more than one unit, but everyone knew which units were "theirs." Despite reorganizations and the addition of conscripts and transfers, there generally remained a core of men serving together who had known each other before the war. The U.S. military recognized and acknowledged community-based recruiting, and later in the war, when the draft was instituted, calculations were made, and localities which had already sent their quota were exempt from the draft.

Largely because of the community-based recruiting, recent immigrants—even those who spoke no English—were able to participate in the war effort. For example, there were units composed of Germanic immigrants to New York whose officers commanded in German, and units of Louisiana recruits whose officers communicated to them in French.

At times, community spirit transcended the unit, and even the army. There are documented instances where brother masons from opposite sides assisted each other, and there were also units composed of freemasons.

Soldiers in community units benefited from the companionship and convenience of serving with fellows they had known before the war. The soldiers knew each other, and so did their families. Letters from the soldiers were sometimes passed around the community, or even published in the local paper.

The soldiers knew each other so well that the identification of the dead was somewhat easier than in units of strangers. Men who knew each other well watched out

Soldiers sometimes pitched in to pay for the embalming of a fellow soldier, quite often a comrade they had known since childhood.

Fencing skills were NOT a prerequisite for Civil War soldiers. These men were undoubtedly "clowning around" for the camera.

for each other in battle, and were often able to recount how and where comrades had fallen, even in the heat of battle.

A down-side to community-based recruiting manifested itself all too often during the Civil War. After major engagements it was not unusual to learn that entire families of fathers and sons, or brothers; or even entire communities had been wiped out. Not until the 20th century did the U.S. military make an effort to forbid this type of recruiting and organization.

Some of the tasks which today are duty items for anonymous military officers were performed instead by personal friends of the soldier. Often soldiers took it upon themselves to notify friends and relatives when a comrade fell. When possible, they arranged for the embalming and/or transport of a body. When it was not possible, they dug graves, and laid in them the bodies of men they had known from childhood. Often, these comrades managed to gather the personal belongings of their comrades. The soldiers kept these items until they

could personally deliver them to the families. Decades after the war, there were soldiers still tracking down the families of their fallen comrades and placing in their hands cherished mementos.

Even an aspiring wealthy man, Lester Frank Ward, was moved to spend some of his wealth contributing to a fund to have a fellow soldier embalmed:

June 19, Sunday
Wednesday I received twenty-six dollars in greenbacks. Friday I gave a dollar to have the body of corporal Saulsbery embalmed and shipped to his mother.[31]

In November of 1862, John French White wrote to his wife in Tidewater:

...Tell Cousin M. I buryed Bro. A the best I could under the circumstances and that I saved all he had of importance about him. I have his money, $192.00, a lock of his hair and a button off his coat which I will bring home to her if it ever be my good fortune to get there.[32]

This is not a female soldier. Rather, it is a young lady so enthusiastic in her support of the war, that she has had a frock coat made for herself with lines similar to those of a soldier.

Sometimes, of course, the community seemed just a bit too close, and soldiers who revealed themselves as cowards could be assured that the entire community would hear of it.

One other result of the community-based recruiting was the close ties which the communities maintained with "their" boys. In the early months, patriotism reached a fever-pitch.

After the initial call for troops, rallies were held in many communities to induce young men to enlist. Infectious enthusiasm and peer pressure induced many a man to enlist. Men, women and children alike attended the rallies.

At one rally in Wisconsin, a young girl became so enthused that she exclaimed (before the entire community) "John, if you do not enlist, I'll never let you kiss me again as long as I live!"[33]

The men and boys may have entertained regrets, but it took a hardy soul to resist the pressure to enlist.

> Soon I these familiar scenes will leave
> Where I, delighted, would ever tarry;
> But duty calls and can I grieve
> For that which I should never parry?
> When far away I think of thee,

Thy sparkling eye and face to pretty,
O sometimes then remember me,
Pining, dying, for Miss Betty.[34]

While the recruits remained in town, parties and festivities were held. When they left, banquets and parades were held in their honor.

May, 1861
Many of the young men are going from Canandaigua and all the neighboring towns. It seems very patriotic and grand when they are singing, "It is sweet, Oh, 'tis sweet, for one's country to die," and we hear the martial music...and meet men in uniform at every turn and see train loads of the boys in blue going to the front, but it will not seem so grand if we hear they are dead on the battlefield, far from home....[35]

In communities where the trains stopped while transporting troops, women cooked, and baked, and fed every hungry soldier they could find. In both north and south, women joined together to make and send off items needed by the soldier. They wrote letters, knitted socks, and prepared and sent packages of foodstuffs. As one young woman recalled,

I well remember the delight it gave us young girls after school to go down Commerce Street to the "aid society" where Mrs. Eliza Moore as president was ever cutting out pants and jackets and overcoats, at first of fine grey cloth and afterwards of homemade jean, almost any muddy color. With the larger "scraps" she would let us cover the bright tin canteens while the more efficient made haversacks of the largest pieces. Others would make the cover, with capes, for the caps of unbleached domestic as a protection from sun and wind.[36]

Mrs. Mary Wade helped to organize and run the Cooper Volunteer Refreshment Saloon in Philadelphia, where soldiers could be assured of a hot meal, and a concerned ear when they stopped over in Philadelphia.

This drawing is one of a series showing facilities for soldiers in New York City. This picture is of the Soldier's Depot and Dining Rooms. Others show laundry and bathing facilities—complete with running water.

Soldiers did not hesitate to request the items they needed,

> ...If you get this before ma sends out the expected-to-be sent package, and if there is some room, you might put in one blanket. Since we sleep two in a bunk, we spread our blankets across the bunk. B has three, and I have three, which makes it equal to six apiece. Send the blanket; it shall do its share of warming, I assure you....[37]

During this initial period of the war—and throughout the long years to come—family members, especially mothers and sweethearts kept up a steady stream of letters to their soldiers. Many a veteran recounted that it was the letters from home which kept up morale, and induced him to keep on even during the darkest days.

> How rightfully the poets say:
> "Home Sweet, Sweet home.
> There is no place like home,
> Let it be ever so humble,
> There is no place like home"[38]

The individual and collective efforts of those who stayed at home, sending socks, supplies and support were universally lauded by those who fought in the war in prose and poetry.

> Camp near Petersburg February 16, 1864
> The members of the third company battalion, Washington Artillery of New Orleans embrace this opportunity of tendering to the "Young Ladies Knitting Society of Fayetteville, NC" their thanks for the recent present of 65 pairs of socks
> "For all the socks the maids have made,
> Our thanks for all the brave,
> And honored be your pious trade,
> The soldier's sole to save."[39]

Those who could not sew, could knit, and those who could not knit, could make preserves, or cut blankets. Parthenia Antoinette Hague must have echoed the experience of many when she wrote "Surely there was work enough to be done."[40]

41

The women of America knitted—and darned—vast quantities of socks for the soldiers.

Civilians

Headquarters Army of Northern Va. After four years of arduous service marked by unsurpassed courage and fortitude, the Army of Northern Virginia has been compelled to yield to overwhelming numbers and resources....[41]

Thus began Robert E. Lee's general order announcing surrender at the end of the war. Today, many historians agree with General Lee's conclusion that his army was largely defeated by its lack of resources. Some have even maintained that once the border states—and the majority of southern manufacturing capability—were lost, the war itself was lost. The surprise, then, is not that the north won the war, but that they took so long to do it.[42]

In war, having skillful soldiers is only half the battle; they must be armed and equipped to fight. Supplies become an important issue in the pursuit of military aims.

In order for supplies to be useful, the army must coordinate three distinct characteristics: It must get the supplies it needs, when it needs them, and where it needs them. The aspect of time—the "when"—was particularly important in the mid-nineteenth century. Technological innovations had brought canned milk and certain other canned products. However, in the absence of large-scale refrigeration, most food, especially meat and vegetables, could not be stored. If transportation was interrupted or unavailable, the food rotted. Animals had to be kept alive and driven to the site where their meat was needed, lest the meat rot before it could be cooked, dried or salted. An army did not need to destroy the other side's food supply; it needed only to delay or prevent its transportation to the troops.

From a supply officer's point of view, the north employed a most effective strategy: While southern armies were winning battles around the capital cities of Richmond, and Washington, northern troops were seizing seaports and enforcing a naval blockade. The U.S. government's western army seized control of much of the Mississippi River. Rail service was disrupted as northern and southern troops fought over major rail centers. The south could not get supplies into the southeastern states by ocean, by river or by rail. Still, the south persevered, growing food and manufacturing clothing within the southeastern states. In the end, the northern armies turned their attention to actually destroying

The four men sitting in the front of this picture are posed with the tools of the tailors; measure tapes, large scissors, and a length of fabric. At military depots, tailors spent their time in cutting and measuring, the sewing was done by seamstresses. The man at the back is probably a foreman.

U.S. Military Railroads were largely staffed by civilian personnel.

southern supplies and manufacturing facilities. When the troops burned their way through the Shenandoah and then through Georgia on Sherman's march to the sea, they were destroying southern food supplies and the ability to produce more in the near future.

But food is not the only necessity of a soldier, the north was assisted in its efforts to defeat the south by the southern economy itself. In America at mid-century, southern society was largely agrarian. The economy of several southern states was based almost exclusively on crops such as tobacco and cotton. The southern armies may have had raw materials and mines, but too few foundries and skilled workers to turn the materials into arms.

The industrial revolution had begun in the north, and in that region, more of the economy was based on manufacturing enterprises. Thus the U.S. government had more facilities at its disposal to manufacture the goods it needed for the troops.

Both armies looked to their civilian populations to supply the goods they needed, with or without adequate manufacturing facilities. To the extent that these civilians were—or were not—able to meet the military's needs, they, too, shared the credit (or blame) for the outcome of the war.

The U.S. Quartermaster warehouse in New Bern, North Carolina, was one of many southern posts that the U.S. government kept supplied through much of the war. In the absence of elevators, a system of pulleys and ropes permitted storage on the upper floors.

Government and other Workers

When the Civil War began, many Americans continued in their pre-war occupations, but supplied the fruits of their efforts to the government, rather than private customers. Among these were the many Americans working on farms, factories and in industries which received government contracts. Men who worked as silversmiths got commissions to make swords. Founders turned from making steam engine boilers to cannon barrels. As the war progressed, and the draft was instituted, managers of armories and foundries made repeated appeals to the military that their skilled workers be exempted from conscription into the military. (This civilian/military conflict is featured in one of the earliest movies about the Civil War: In *The General*, Buster Keaton, who wants to join the military, is prevented from doing so because the railroad needs his skills as an engineer.)

Others found employment in working directly for the government as civilians. Government workshops employed people to construct and repair the wagons, caissons, and pontoon bridges which the armies spent their time alternately building and destroying. Men and women alike were employed at ammunition factories, and these were jobs that were not without danger. At Browns Island in Richmond, Virginia, a young woman working with friction primers hit a primer with her shoe to loosen it, and blew up the building in which she was working. She lived long enough to tell her story, but soon died of her wounds.

Military personnel at depots in the north and the south purchased miles of fabric, and issued millions of martial garments, yet their are few indications that uniforms were manufactured in government facilities. Sewing for the depots was a cottage industry. Cut fabric and measured trims were issued to tens of thousands of civilian seamstresses who manufactured the clothing and were paid on a per-piece basis. Given the system, it is perhaps remarkable that military clothing for the period shows the consistency that it does.

Government efforts to obtain supplies sometimes outstripped their ability to monitor the quality of the

This Office of the U.S. Depot of Army Clothing and Equipage was located in buildings built for the purpose in Washington, DC.

One of many government saw mills that provided wood timbers for the army.

This office of Government Repair Shops was located in Washington, DC. It would appear that the entire staff posed for the picture.

46

This entrepreneur advertised on his cart that he carried newspapers from Philadelphia, New York, and Baltimore.

supplies. While most firms employed in the war industry sought to produce quality goods, there were some who took advantage of the lack of oversight in government contracts. There were also times when any goods—however defective—were better than none at all.

> ...But the troops were clothed and rescued from severe suffering and those who saw the sentinels walking post about the Capital of the US. in freezing weather in their drawers, without trousers or overcoats, will not blame the department for its efforts to clothe them, even in materials not quite so durable as army blue kersey....[43]

The cost of the goods, whether shoddy or excellent, far outstripped either government's resources. In the north, the first income tax was instituted to help pay for the war.[44] In the south, the government issued bonds to investors who gambled that their new government would reward loyalty.

The photograph album containing this image identified the man as a steam boat captain for the U.S. army, but regrettably did not list his name.

The U.S. Sanitary and Other Commissions

In the first year of the war, a group of civilians approached Abraham Lincoln with an idea for helping out in the war effort. He dismissed their suggestion with the comment that the buggy did not need a "fifth wheel." Eventually, however, he was persuaded to approve the formation of the United States Sanitary Commission for the purpose of supplementing—but not supplanting—the efforts of the government. It was given special responsibility for the health and welfare of soldiers.

The Sanitary Commission is perhaps best known for its fund-raising efforts. Members of the Commission took projects which had been successful on a local level, and raised them to a national level. Organizers of Sanitary Fairs—and other events to raise funds for the relief of soldiers—were creative in their approach, and masters at capitalizing on interest in the war.

One of the civilian volunteers who helped to provide for the health and welfare of wounded soldiers was Walt Whitman.

The "Sanitary Fairs" held in Philadelphia and other locations featured exhibits of firearms, flags, and items captured in battle, as well needlework and preserves. The United States Sanitary Commission was quite possibly the first group to present a re-enactment of a Civil War battle, complete with reproduction weapons, to the public:

> ...A portion of the Frog Pond was shut in and covered by a tent with a platform running round it for the spectators. Upon the sheet of water thus enclosed there came out a little *Merrimac*, propelled by steam, which, as I remember, rammed and sank two representatives of the *Cumberland* and *Congress*. Then out darted the *Monitor*, and there was much firing of the little guns until the *Merrimac* was withdrawn, sinking and crippled.

Henry Cabot Lodge, who described the event in his *Early Memories* noted that the narrator for the event was Edward Everett, the distinguished orator.[45]

For the Maryland State Fair (Baltimore, 1864), Mrs. Amos Binney persuaded several top-ranking Generals of the Union army, and the President of the United States to contribute official documents of significance which were sold at the fair for the benefit of the Commission.

The Commission also sold items relating to the war. Like many women, Sarah M. Broadhead kept a journal. Hers is of particular interest because she was living in Gettysburg at the time of the battle there. Shortly after the battle, 200 copies of Sarah's diary for the period were published, and 75 of these were given to the Sanitary Commission for the 1864 Sanitary Fair in Philadelphia.[46]

Aside from fund-raising, the Sanitary Commission became involved in a broad range of issues relating to the health and welfare of soldiers. The Commission had its roots in the sanitary movement which had emerged in Europe during the 1840s and 50s. Members of the sanitary movement subscribed to the innovative theory that disease was environmental. Taking note of experiences during the recent Crimean War, the U.S. Sanitary Commission sent representatives to inspect camps and ensure that they were situated and arranged near clean, running water, and that efforts were made to minimize the spread of disease.

In the area of "welfare," the Commission distributed medical necessities and coordinated the efforts of the thousands of women who were sending packages of supplies to the soldiers. In the beginning, the uncoordinated voluntary system had worked very well; soldiers wrote home, asking for the items they needed, and their families sent them. Local "ladies' aid societies" in many communities manufactured quantities of items to send off to "their" soldiers. Very quickly, logistical problems developed. Boxes were damaged en-route, and some soldiers received more than they needed, while others went without.

The Sanitary Commission was the largest, but certainly not the only, organization which took action to help relieve some of the many problems facing the soldiers.

The Christian Commission, which was largely financed by church groups, also collected and distributed items to soldiers, and helped to set up, supply, and staff hospitals. One major difference between the two is that the Christian Commission sought to save the soldier's soul, as well as his body, and often offered "prayers with the porridge."

Many accounts by the soldiers contain glowing accounts of heroic deeds of the commissions. However, their efforts were not always appreciated:

August 22nd
...We came alongside the wharf at Jersey City...On shore we were instantly besieged by a small army of Agents of the Christian Commission who seemed to entertain the reprehensible idea that we were from some remote part of the world where the light of civilization has never dawned, instead of from puritanical New England where Bibles are as plentiful as dogs in an Irish

Many, many efforts were made to raise money for the war effort. In some communities, fairs, bazaars, and theatricals were held.

neighborhood. They insisted on giving each of us a Testament although there isn't a man among us who hasn't one already from home. No doubt they judged us by the New Yorkers who have gone to the front....[47]

These comments were far from ordinary, as most had nothing but praise for the Christian Commission, and the Sanitary Commission. In Sarah M. Broadhead's Gettysburg diary, she lauded the efforts of both the Sanitary Commission, and the Christian Commission.

The merciful work of the Sanitary and Christian Commissions, aided by private contributions, was to be seen at every hospital. Without the relief they furnished, thousands must have perished miserably, and thousands more have suffered from want of the delicacies, food and clothing their agents distributed, before the Government even could bring assistance. They are God's blessed agencies for providing for the needy soldier.[48]

There is one other area in which civilian volunteers—and the Sanitary and Christian Commissions—became involved with the war: medical. A much-increased need for medical care is a by-product of war. Adequate medical care for the soldiers was largely a problem of logistics; immediately after a battle doctors, nurses and medical supplies were needed—fast. The need continued for days, weeks, and even months, until the last soldier convalesced.

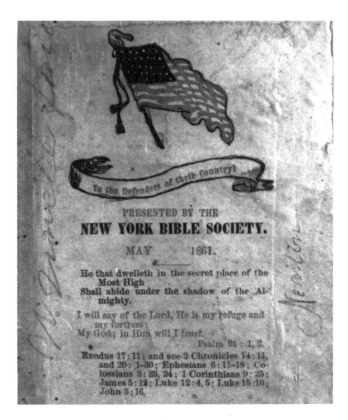

Frontpiece of a bible presented to soldiers.

Medical Supplies and Care

Both northern and southern governments enlisted doctors into the military and also hired contract surgeons. Nurses were often soldiers unfit for combat duties. However, the need for medical care was far greater than anticipated, therefore, civilians stepped in. A careful reading of contemporary accounts reveals that most of those who "worked in the hospitals" spent far more time meeting the human needs of the soldiers—both physical and mental—than in providing medical care. Civilians stepped in to take care of tasks like collecting and distributing supplies and food, keeping records, cleaning, and communicating with soldiers' relatives and friends.

The Woolsey family of New York is an example of the sort of enthusiastic participation with which some responded to the war. All eight children of Charles William and Jane Woolsey found a way to participate in the war. This is not a unique occurrence; there were many families which sent several sons to fight. The remarkable feature of the Woolsey family participation is that seven of the eight children were females. Several of the daughters worked in hospitals, including Eliza Woolsey Howland, who wrote the following:

...One of the first...hospitals of the war was in the top story of the Patent Office. The great, unfinished lumber room was set aside...and rough tables—I can't call them beds—were knocked together from pieces of the scaffolding. These beds were so high that it was impossible to reach them, and we had to make them up with brooms, sweeping off the mattresses....As the number [of patients] increased, camp beds were set up between the glass cases in the outer room, and we alternated—typhoid fever, cog wheels and patent churns—typhoid fever, balloons and mouse traps (How many ways of catching mice there are!)—typhoid fever, locomotives, water wheels, clocks....

Gradually, out of the confusion came some system and order. Climbing up to the top of the Patent Office with each loaf of bread was found not to be an amusing occupation, and an arrangement of pulleys was made out of one of the windows, and any time through the day, barrels of water, baskets of vegetables, and great pieces of army beef might be seen crawling slowly up the marble face of the building.[49]

The U.S. Patent Office building in Washington was used as a hospital during the Civil War. "[A]ny time through the day, barrels of water, baskets of vegetables, and great pieces of army beef might be seen crawling slowly up the marble face of the building."

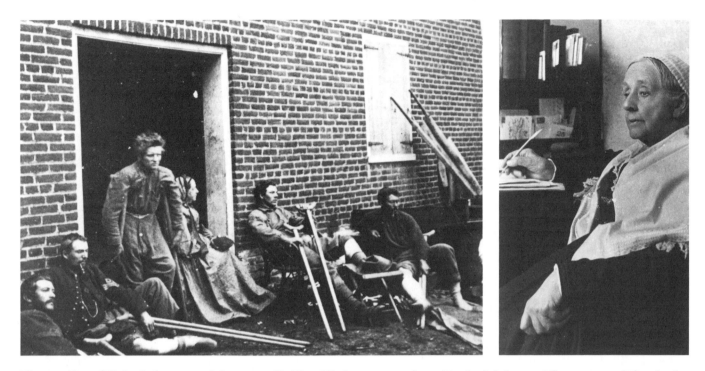

The much-published photograph is generally identified as a scene from Fredericksburg. The woman sitting in the doorway is seldom, if ever, identified. She is Mrs. A.M. Gibbons, who served her country at Washington, Falls Church, Winchester, Strasburg, Point Lookout, Fredericksburg, White House and City Point. She survived all of these experiences, and the second photograph was taken much later in her life.

Civilians took on every task from stirring soup to managing supplies. Hospital logistics were very often left to the matrons of the hospitals. The degree to which a hospital did—or did not—run smoothly, depended on the matron's management abilities, and (often) her ability to work with the military command structure.

In addition to the many civilians who performed non-medical tasks, there were some who joined surgeons and orderlies in actually laying hands on the wounded soldiers. In the south, women relied on their early training and life experience, but in the north, official training was provided to the nurses accepted by Dorothea Dix into "her" official nurse corps.

Secretary of War Stanton was persuaded of the need to use women in nursing positions, and appointed Dorothea Dix to a position in which she had complete control over the selection, training, and assignment of all women nurses employed by the army. Miss Dix has been criticized for her dictatorial management techniques, and her seemingly arbitrary decisions. She required that nurses be homely and plainly dressed, turning away those who were too young, or well endowed. Miss Dix had reasons for her concern about the morals of those who would volunteer for nursing duty: In America at mid-century, there was generally only one group of women—outside of Catholic nuns—who had experi-ence in nursing outside their homes. They were con-victed prostitutes who, in some jurisdictions, were given the option of serving their sentences in jails or working in hospitals.

Miss Dix appointed Dr. Elizabeth Blackwell, America's "first" female graduate of an accredited medical school, to set up a program for training the nurses. Dr. Blackwell's behind-the-scenes role in the war has been largely forgotten. Blackwell was unlike Dr. Mary Elizabeth Walker, who actually ministered to the troops and won a Medal of Honor for her efforts. In general, the role which women played in providing medical care met with rave reviews.

> ...The great Father knew whether the male or the female would make the best nurse, when He gave her, instead of him, the care of infants and children.[50]

A relatively small—but much noted—group of civil-ians provided medical care on the field of battle. Even those who traveled to the battle sites generally cared for the sick and dying in temporary hospitals which were set up in barns, and houses near the battlefields. Their tasks did not end when the armies marched off to the next campaign, or the next battle. Instead, the care for the wounded continued for months afterwards.

Other Civilian Participation

Medical care is not the only area in which civilians were able to help the military. Soldiers spent most of their time living in military camps or moving from one place to another—and only a small portion actually fighting battles. It follows, then, that civilians found opportunities for assisting soldiers during those less dramatic times. In addition to those who worked in defense industries, and those who helped with medical care, there were those with personal talents who saw a need, and filled it.

E.W. Locke, for example, filled a role much like that of Bob Hope in the twentieth century. Like Hope, Locke helped the army to maintain morale by entertaining the troops. Unlike Hope, Locke's shows were small, simple

Several photographers followed the army, providing America with immediate—and often gruesome—images of the aftermath of battles. Other photographers set up near camps, providing soldiers with images to send home.

Many women helped in the war efforts. Louisa May Alcott volunteered at a hospital in the Georgetown area of Washington, DC. While there, she caught a fever which rendered her an invalid for life. Years later, she commented on her experience:
"I never have regretted that brief yet costly experience. All that is best and greatest in the hearts of men and women comes out at times like those, and the courage, loyalty, fortitude and self-sacrifice I saw and learned to love and admire in both northern and southern soldiers can never be forgotten."

song-fests, his accompaniment just what the soldiers themselves could play. It was an unpaid, and unofficial, position, but Locke was able to support himself by selling sheet music and song sheets. After the war, he published a book of his songs and experiences, but like Benvenuto Celini, his memoir remains while his fame has faded.

> This book is published more especially for friends and acquaintances, many of whom may be found in nearly every town in the Northern and Western States. Having met with most of the "boys in blue" in the Army...it will be seen that, for a man of medium gifts, I am very extensively known.[51]

There are accounts of women who followed their soldiers to war, serving as "mothers" to all, cooking, cleaning and laundering for one or another company of soldiers. A few of the women, like Mary Bickerdyke—laundress, hospital matron, nurse and mother figure—became legends in their own time. Others published books about their experiences, but the vast majority afterwards returned to lives of quiet anonymity.

> We did not go to the war for money or praise. When I went it was a horrid affair....I was independent of all Commissions. My Regiment, the glorious old Second New Hampshire was enough for me.[52]

This carte de visite of Sergeant MacNutty (standing, right) and two others was published and sold by the U.S. Sanitary Commission to raise funds as the backmark above shows.

In the interest of accuracy, it must also be noted that *filles de joie*—campfollowers and prostitutes—gathered in cities and towns where quantities of soldiers were housed for any period of time. The area of Washington, DC, today known as Federal Triangle was a center of criminal and illicit activities. In 1863, police made a concerted effort to clean out the area by rounding up prostitutes and criminals. They marched them to the railroad station, where they strongly encouraged them to board trains leaving town. If the program did not prove successful, it was at least done with a certain flair. On the march to the railroad station, a brass band accompanied the parade playing "The Rogue's March."[53]

There were also a few women who disguised themselves as men and fought alongside the soldiers. The contributions of these female soldiers to the war effort are generally considered insignificant. At the time, these women were not generally admired.

The practice of selling artifacts to raise money continued during and after the war. This photograph shows a display of relics from Andersonville Prison. Clara Barton sold them at a fair in Washington, DC, in 1866.

Some have identified this as a portrait of a Yankee laundress. She may have served as a laundress. The children, dog, and cooking equipment probably indicate that she was one of the women who joined her husband at his military camp. The presence of the tent implies that this was not an army "on the march."

We did not go to war for money or praise.
—Harriet C. Dada

I have no one to send—I'll go myself, and nurse the sick.

Detail from a patriotic envelope of the period.

...We sent away to Fort McHenry another...female woman clad so snugly in a soldier's uniform.... This one...was by no means an "ornament to her sex." On the whole she was a rather scaly looking specimen of a human, has a face similar to a crocodile and a voice as sweet as an old cow bell....[54]

E. W. Locke, who maintained that he had met most of the "Boys in Blue" entitled one chapter of his book "Women in the Army." He then began the chapter by stating that he had seen women slaving over kettles, and cooking turnovers, and he had seen the eagle of the Wisconsin regiment,

...[B]ut I do not recollect to have seen a single specimen of this poetic character, "La Fille du Regiment." It is said there was a woman with the first Michigan Cavalry, who was known as Irish Biddy; but if there was, she wore the dress, did the work, and drew the pay of a soldier."[55]

Today, the masculine women-soldiers are held in high esteem, a development more indicative of modern culture, than of the opinions at the time of the war.

Not all women working in hospitals were nurses. From November 1862 until August 1865, Mrs. Anna Lowell of Old Cambridge, Massachusetts was in charge of a special diet kitchen at Armory Square Hospital in Washington.

Chapter V
The Effect of War on Civilian Life

After the smoke cleared in early July 1863, the two great armies of Robert E. Lee and George G. Meade moved away from the little town of Gettysburg. They headed toward the South Mountain and two more grim years of war that would lead to Appomattox. And they left the citizens of the town to deal with the reality of what the armies had wrought.

Their experience brought home the reality of the conflict to the north as never before. Perhaps for the first time, northern families got a close up look at the war and its impact. The citizens of Gettysburg cleaned up, buried the dead, cared for the wounded, repaired the damage and tried to bring a sense of normalcy back into their lives. They soon came to realize that the change in their town from a small quiet, farming community to a battlefield site with an international reputation was permanent.

Never again would Gettysburg be quite like the thousands of other small American towns that were quiet, close-knit communities. By an accident of history, Gettysburg became not only a turning point of the war, but a symbol of the impact of war on the ordinary citizen.

There were, of course, thousands of other places, mostly in the south, where the psychological and physical impact of the war touched the civilians of America in a direct and brutal way. In Atlanta, Columbia and Richmond, at Culpeper Courthouse and Warrenton, Virginia, at Vicksburg, Mississippi, and Chambersburg, Pennsylvania, and at farm after farm wherever the soldiers marched through—or stayed and camped—the war brought physical destruction.

Even those who had ardently and enthusiastically supported the war at its outset changed their minds when the realities of war began destroying lives.

> Yes, I hate soldiers.
>
> I can't help writing it—it relieves my mind. All morning we have been driving about that horrid region into which our beautiful [county] has been transmogrified; round and round, up and down, in at the south camp and out at the north camp; directed hither and thither by muddle-headed privates; stared at by puppyish young officers; choked with chimney-smoke; jolted over roads laid with sashes—or no roads at all—and pestered everywhere with the sight of lounging, lazy...groups...What a treat it is to get home and lock myself in my own room...and spurt out my wrath in the blackest of ink with the boldest of pens.[56]

When Dinah Maria Muloch Craig wrote these words as the opening paragraph of her novel, *A Life for a Life*, she was writing about the Crimean War. The thoughts she expressed were echoed only a decade later by Americans who quickly grew tired of the Civil War.

June 9

...When we read of the battles in India, in the Crimea, what did we care? It was only an interesting topic, like any other, to look for in the paper. Now...It has come home to us. Half the people that we know in the world are under the enemy's guns....[57]

While it is certainly true that the war had different effects in different parts of the country, it was a rare American who did not grow tired of four years of death and destruction.

Sarah Preston Hale a Boston matron, showed herself a master of understatement when she wrote in her journal: "January 1, 1863, [we are] so prosperous and so little changed. It must be all so different in the South!"[58]

General Lee established his headquarters near this stone building during the Battle of Gettysburg. Lee may have dined here at what was then the residence of the widow Mary Thompson. Still a home in the 1880s when this photo was taken, today the house contains a museum and gift shop. The building's transformation from an anonymous, country building, to museum and tourist attraction reflects the transformation which has taken place for much of Gettysburg itself.

War Affected Families

Mary Englesby was a 13-year old girl living in Wisconsin in 1861. As the men of her community prepared to march off to war, she decided to find a soldier with whom she might correspond. John F. Brobst, a former suitor of Mary's aunt agreed. Brobst wrote her candid letters about the damage he and other soldiers did to the southern farms they visited.

> The people up north do not know what war is. If they were to come down here once, they would soon find out the horror of war. Wherever the army goes, they leave nothing behind them, take all the horses, all the cattle hogs, sheep, chickens, corn and in fact, everything, the longer the rebs hold out the worse it is for them.[59]

Fun & Fury 5 Drops
Residences, churches, and other civilian buildings were not immune to military vandalism and damage.

This family strolls through deserted streets lined with abandoned buildings. Families had to make tough decisions between abandoning their homes to the coming armies, or staying and taking personal risks.

This photograph is identified as "Mrs. Allsop's House." There is no word of whether Mrs. Allsop appreciated the rooftop addition, or how she felt about having a sentry posted over her front hall.

In the north and the south families were first effected by the war when their brothers, sons and father marched away, even for the short enlistments which were offered at the outset of the war. Many who did not wish to be away from their families for long periods of time accepted the 90- and 120-day assignments, then returned home. It was not an acceptable arrangement from the government's point of view, as officers found that they would just get the soldiers trained, when they were released to go back home. When the short enlistments were over, the armies on both sides switched to one- and two-year enlistments. In the final years of the war, draft and enlistment terms required that the soldiers remain in the military for three years or the duration of the war.

The lengthy enlistments caused great hardship for many families, who needed their men to plant, or harvest, or carry on other business. In many families, women took on more visible roles in the finances and family businesses than they previously held. For example: Frank "Bull" Paxton had lived in Rockbridge County,

Virginia, all his life. To support his family, he ran a farm in the country, and a struggling law practice in town. In his letters, Paxton includes much advice on how his wife should handle the business while he is gone.

> I have not time to think of my business at home. My duties now for my State require every energy of mind and body which I can devote to them. Do just as you please. If you think proper stay in town and leave all matters and keys on the farm in charge of John Fitzgerald.

> I hope you are having good success as a farmer; so, if I should be left behind when the war is over, you may be able to take care of yourself....

> The horse trade was entirely satisfactory. Act in the same way in all matters connected with the farm. Just consider yourself a widow, and in military parlance, insist upon being "obeyed and respected accordingly."[60]

It was good practice. Less than two years later, Elizabeth White Paxton no longer had to act as a widow: She became a real one when General William "Bull"

Paxton was killed while leading his men in a charge at the Battle of Chancellorsville.

Not all families had a choice in the matter of letting women run the family business. Men who had worked for wages deprived their families of that income when they went off to war.

In the modern army, the government tries to ease the impact of a soldier's absence from the family. Pay checks can be sent directly home. Military families are offered special arrangements for buying food and obtaining medical care. During the Civil War, however, this was not the case. Soldiers were paid in cash, in the field, and on an extremely irregular schedule. In the months between pay musters, the soldiers' families had no income.

Bermuda Hundred, VA Aug. 22, 1864

The great excitement in the army is now about pay. Half the men in our Regiment are men of families and most of them depend on their wages to support their families.

On the first of September most of the army will have six months' pay due them. Men here receive letters every day that their families are suffering for want of money, but we can't get the pay, for the Government says it hasn't got the money. It requires a mighty sight of patriotism to keep a man's spirit up under such circumstances.[61]

Once paid, the soldier often had no safe way of sending the money home. This was such a problem that the Governor of Indiana helped to earn his nickname "friend to the soldier" by hiring individuals who provided safe transport of the soldiers' pay to their families in Indiana.

Unlike wars fought by Americans in the twentieth century, the Civil War took place on American soil. When the armies advanced and took this town, or that hillside, they were American towns and hillsides, and they were occupied by American citizens. As long as the military occupied an area, civilians experienced something new: life under military rule.

Anne S. Frobel [who endured so much destruction to her family home] continued to keep her diary through 1878. She and her sister, Lizzie, lived in poverty for the rest of their lives. Frobel accepted the defeat of her government, but considered herself an innocent victim of the war. As such, she repeatedly applied to the U.S. government for compensation for damages done to Wilton Hill. She made the impolitic mistake of having her claim pressed by her brother, who had been an officer in the Confederate army. The Frobel request would probably have been denied even if brother Bushrod had not submitted it. The U.S. government carefully screened all requests for pensions and other claims for any evidence that the requestors had been southern sympathizers. Frobel had made little attempt to hide her sentiments during the war. The U.S. government did not provide pensions to Confederate soldiers, and they did not generally honor the claims of southern sympathizers. Indeed, great efforts were made to ensure that individuals who had been disloyal could be identified. The government compiled—and still retains—the military records of those who fought for the south, and a "Citizens and Businesses" file of civilians with any known connection to the Confederate government.

In the end, Mrs. Frobel's claim was denied. "O life, life! What have we to live for? It is only a struggle day after day to keep body and soul together."

Civil and Human Rights: Rescinded by the War

Many Americans in 1861 could recall the participation of their ancestors in the Revolutionary War, some four score years earlier. The new national Constitution, adopted in 1787, had amended to it a Bill of Rights—to guarantee the basic rights and liberties of the people. The progression from the "Bill of Rights" to life under military rule must have seemed a giant step backwards.

Several of the rights specifically protected in the "Bill of Rights" were rescinded for those Americans living under military rule. Travel, communication and commerce were all restricted, and civilians could be forced to carry a pass to take trips as simple as going to the town to shop at the market—if there was anything to buy.

County courthouses and government buildings were invaded by soldiers, who sometimes scattered files and records to the four winds. This photograph of the Charles City County Courthouse in central Virginia shows papers laying about on the lawn.

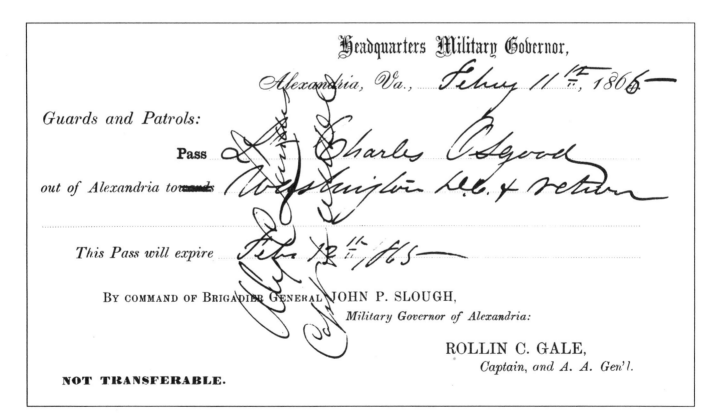

Military, as well as civilian, personnel were required to have passes in order to travel unmolested. This pass permitted Private Charlie Osgood to travel out of Alexandria to Washington and return.

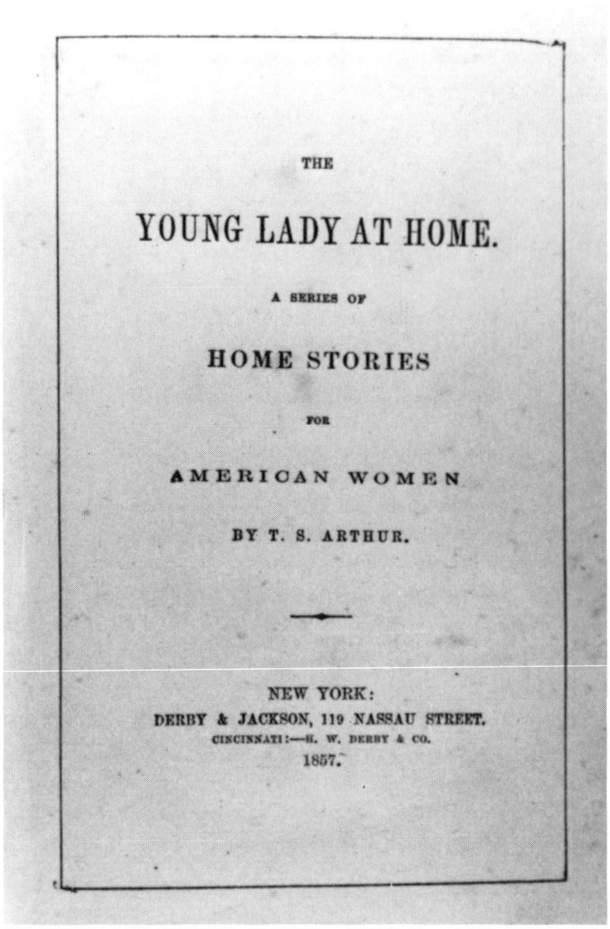

Even soldiers who meant no harm sometimes left unsettling evidence of their visits. One soldier inscribed a book found in a home in New Market, Maryland, then left the book for its rightful owner:

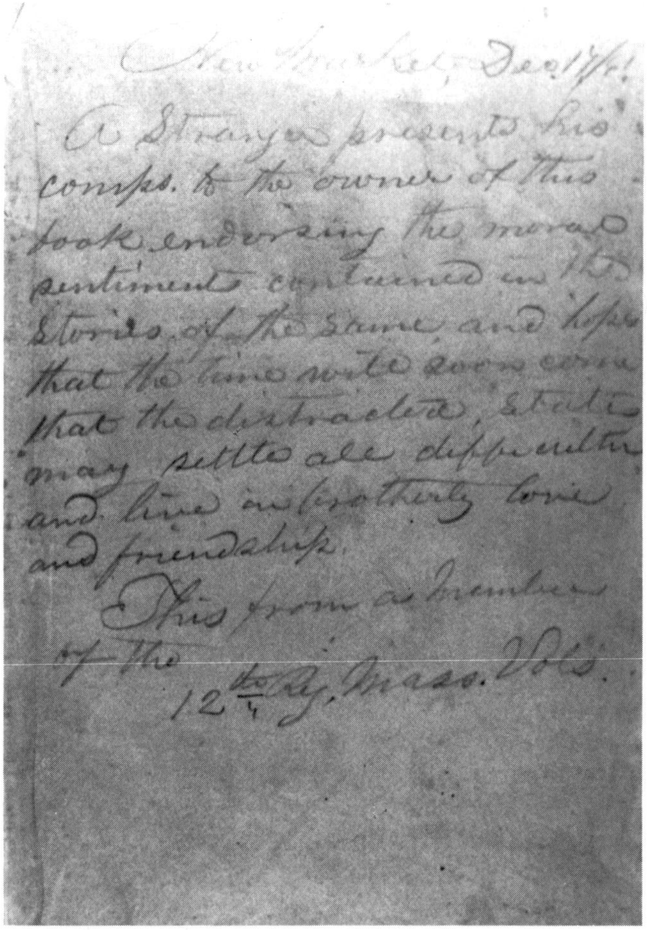

New Market, Dec. 17/61

A Stranger presents his comps. to the owner of this book endorsing the moral sentiments contained in the stories of the same and hopes that the time will soon come that the distracted states may settle all difficulties and live in brotherly love and friendship.

This from a member of the

12th Reg., Mass. Vols.

Civilians also found the lack of reliable information to be a trial. With the military controlling much of the news, citizens could not rely on the reports which they received, even about battles which took place nearby. As a result, erroneous information abounded.

Anne Frobel related in her diary how she first heard about the Battle of Balls Bluff, which took place within thirty miles of her home:

...Mrs. Dawsy, Mrs. Fairfax's mother who is very fanciful about her eating, as all old people are said, "have you any salt fish, last year's fish, do pray if you have send me some...."O" she said "I am so hungry for fish and I can't eat what they bring from market, I know they have been so many months fattening on the dead yankees in the river."

I repeated "dead yankees in the river," how did they get there.

"Why," she said "have you never heard of the battle of Ball's Bluff fought as far back as last May, where our boys drove the yankees into the Potomac by hundreds and thousands and nearly drowned the whole army, and the tide has been throwing them up on the banks and they have been fishing out the dead men ever since" ...And this was the first we had heard of the battle of Ball's Bluff.[62]

Interestingly, the above quote is a double example of erroneous, late and confused information. The Battle of Ball's Bluff was actually fought on October 21, 1861!

Civilians complained bitterly about the military occupations, but learned to live under and within the system. Some civilians found that they could apply to the Provost for a guard who would —theoretically—protect their homes from intrusion by renegade soldiers. In at least one case, a civilian was able to take advantage of the need for passes in order to foil an attempt by one of his daughters to elope with a soldier.[63]

Mostly, those living under military rule had little good to say about it; even innocent children and infants were victims. One civilian enduring the inconvenience of life under military rule related an incident in which Union troops temporarily blockaded a road. The blockade stopped all traffic, and prevented several women from going home to feed their small infants. There was no evidence of the enemy, and one woman could actually see her house from where she was on the road.

> She was sitting in the buggy...she pointed out her house, and begged and entreated to be allowed to go to her infant. ...[A]t last she became so exasperated she vowed she would go, and out of the buggy she jumped and over the fence, and half way the field before the wretch who was running after caught her, she pulled and pushed and tusseled with him and at last got away and off again through the field, and through the yard, up the steps and across the porch and into the front door and dashed it in his face.[64]

As war continued, citizens—at least in the south—began to see the devastation and disaster, and to feel the impact of war. In his travels with the army, entertainer E. W. Locke noted the destruction done to civilians:

> ...The army lived much better than the citizens among whom it quartered. The poorer class of the South, before the war, never lived so well as the same class North. ...During the war, many of the Southern people were reduced almost to starvation....[65]

"Wilton Hill" was an estate in Fairfax County, Virginia. At the time of the war, Anne and Lizzie Frobel, two maiden sisters lived at this, their family home. They had one brother, who joined the Confederate army. Anne Frobel kept a diary which is largely a litany of complaints against the Yankees, who camped at Wilton Hill for several years during the war. Frobel noted in great detail the destruction of her family home, lock, stock, and barrel. She documented the theft of everything from fireplace mantles to laundry from the line. Frobel would not have agreed that she was fortunate, but she was at least left with a roof over her head, if not with food to eat, or water to drink, or the wood to heat her house. She included in her diary many incidents perpetrated on the southern-sympathizing residents of Fairfax County,

Virginia:

> July 1861 [Miss Emily Davis, a neighbor, reported that...] they searched and plundered the house from garret to cellar, then they went out and hitched up the carriages, wagons, carts, everything they could find, killed the horses, mules and cows. There were none but ladies, children and servants...Miss Betsy is old and infirm. The violence, noise, and oaths...alarmed her so that she gave way as if in a fainting fit...paralysis ensued, and never from that hour to the day of her death did she utter one coherent sentence.

> They take or destroy everything they can lay their hands upon. Sometimes the poor cows come home dripping with blood where they have been shot, or stuck with bayonets....

> [A soldier related that]...at one poor miserable old log house when they found one woman and a house full of poor starved looking little children, they tried to make her tell where her husband was, but could get nothing

It might be tempting to believe that the photographer caught two soldiers in the act of stealing this animal. However, the backmark of the photograph indicates that it was taken at "Geisboro, District of Columbia." At the time, Geisboro (now Blue Plains) was a remount station for the U.S. Army. The photograph was probably taken as an editorial comment on the quality of horses being provided to the cavalry.

out of her. They drove her cow off and then looked round to see what eatables they could find, but there was nothing on earth to be found, but a small patch of turnips in the garden, the soldiers flew into that and tore them all out of the ground and all they could not eat or carry off, they threw away. Then he imitated the poor woman's ignorant talk and her crying, and her begging and imploring that her turnips and cow might be left to her as they were her only means of feeding her children. They all laughed very much at this witty recital.[66]

The plight of civilians who had been driven from their homes touched the hearts of Quaker schoolmistresses living in South Carolina just after the war.

...[W]e learned from her that she was a refugee from Plymouth. She lost her house...at the time of our recent taking of Plymouth. The tears stood in her eyes while she talked about it; but she controlled herself sublimely.

"My sister and I are not keeping house in Newberne," she said, "because we have nothing to keep house with," and the tears came again, but she looked a queen, all the while....[67]

The Quaker schoolmistresses related the damage done to Bruton Parish Church, in Williamsburg, Virginia.

...At the head of Main St. stand the ruins of William and Mary's College...Halfway down the pretty street, a desolated church faces the desolate court-house and government horses are stabled in the basement of each [building]....The rebels removed the pews, and made of the church a hospital. "We tried to prevent them," the sexton said, "but they excised." "This house was once a house of grace, now disease and sickness fills the place," said the sexton.[68]

"The Sacking of Fredericksburg" was drawn by Aurthur Lumly on December 12, 1862, and it illustrates Union soldiers looting private homes and businesses.

The Blockade: A Military and Civilian Scourge

One of the military strategies employed during the war was the practice of depriving the enemy of supplies. The northern armies were particularly effective at this, and the blockade which they enforced did deprive southern troops of much-needed arms. However, the blockade also restricted the transportation of food, clothing, medical supplies and other goods which were needed by civilians as well as soldiers. As the blockade tightened, shortages developed throughout the south.

Southern literature abounds with information on the sometimes ingenious substitutions which were made. Southerners turned local plants into coffee, dye, food, tea, and quite a number of medicines which were claimed to be just as effective as the "real" compounds. In place of manufactured dry-goods, southern women went to their attics, and pulled out long-idle looms on which they re-learned the art of weaving homespun threads into fabrics.

Parthenia Antoinette Hague was a young lady living in Alabama at the time of the Civil War. Shortly after the war, Hague published a book which detailed her life in the blockaded south.

> All in our settlement learned to card, spin and weave, and that was the case with all the women of the South when the blockade closed us in....Our days of novitiate were short....[69]

All the experiments were not successful.

> ...[O]ne of our acquaintances...set out to excel us, in that she ...was herself going to weave the thread she had spun into cloth for her dress....Her homespun warp proved to be quite defective. ...She became impatient and wearied at the oft-breaking threads ...and by the time she had woven three or four yards she had tired altogether of mending and piecing....She kept on weaving, however, but the more threads that broke the fewer there were there to sustain the remaining cones, so that the cloth, from being a good yard wide at the beginning, narrowed to less than half a foot, and after the first two or three yards was useless for any purpose.[70]

Parthenia Antoinette Hague noted in her account of life in blockaded Alabama that the women in her community knitted shawls for themselves, competing to see who could devise the most ornate border pattern. The backmark does not indicate that this woman is from Alabama, but her knitted shawl certainly has a bold border.

Refugees: Those Made Homeless by the War

Women like Miss Frobel, who complained of her cows being bayonetted, saw destruction from living in an occupied area. Blockaded women like Miss Hague, saw substitution. However, it was those made homeless by the war; refugees like Mrs. James M. Loughborough, who struggled with some of the most difficult circumstances. Mrs. Loughborough even tried living in a cave in the hillside near Vicksburg, Mississippi.

In the face of an advancing army, civilians faced the dilemma of staying in their homes and risking their lives, or leaving their homes and risking the homes' destruction. Civilians in battle- or camp-areas generally understood that houses standing empty would be ransacked, and very often, destroyed. The civilians could ask for protection, and risk being thought sympathizers with whichever army was occupying the area but many then feared that when the military left, they would be ostracized or criticized by their neighbors.

At times, the shortages became desperate. Mrs. Loughborough related that a soldier had given her young daughter a bird to play with. When they ran entirely out of food, the pet was killed and cooked that the girl might have a meal.[71]

Homes in enemy occupied areas or in the path of battling armies were often ransaked and severely damaged.

This photograph of the Shirley or "white" house has been titled "the Caves of Vicksburg," but it does not show the caves in which civilians like Mrs. Loughborough hid. Rather, this was a portion of the Union siege line where soldiers of the 45th Illinois constructed their own bombproof shelters.

A refugee family crossing the Rappahannock River with their possessions loaded onto an ox cart.

67

The Tragedy of War

The loss of a home, and earthly possessions, or even a pet pales by comparison to other results of the war. The horror of war is not in the destruction of property, but in the destruction of bodies and lives.

When soldiers enlisted in the military, many left their families for the first time in their lives. The anxiety of separation was felt keenly by the soldiers.

Married men who were separated from their families had many concerns. They worried that infants born while they were away might die before they ever saw them, or that some other tragedy would befall them. John French White suffered over leaving his wife, Mattie, and young daughter, Orah:

Richmond, May 19, 1862

...I am thinking [of]...the morning of my departure. O, memorable morning, I often think of it, and me now thinks I can see my little darling O, as I stooped to kiss and tell her good-bye, turn off reluctantly, much as to say Papa I don't want to tell you good-bye, I don't want you to go, and then arising and approaching the spot where you stood, my watery eyes falling upon yours already bedimmed with tears....[72]

Although White regularly sent messages to Orah in his letters to his wife Mattie, he worried that Orah would forget him. His fears were not unfounded. As he recounted a trip home on furlough, his sadness is apparent.

Petersburg Mar 21, 1863

My Very Dear Mat,
...Dear I am thinking now of my visit to see you....I tapped at the glass...the door was open....How ardent our greetings, and when it was over, and I had spoken to Seth; you remember who I next sought, but she was asleep, I could not help it; I waked her up. Did she know me? Ah, no. Time and senses had removed me far from her precious little mind. But I promised to be brief on this subject....[73]

Soldiers heard their loved ones calling them, and yet most stayed in the military, continuing the fight, even when they wanted desperately to go home. The soldiers were painfully aware of the suffering their families experienced as a result of war. One soldier described the death scene of his comrades:

...Men wounded in every manner imaginable. Some dead, others dying...Some cursing the war that deprived

A legend which accompanies this photograph states that the man is holding the very cannonball that took off both his legs. Men who suffered physical—and mental—effects of the war often had a difficult time in readjusting to life as civilians.

them of a leg or an arm and made them cripples for life, and in the same breath praying for their families who were suffering and, they knew, must always suffer by reason of it.[74]

Many soldiers thought of their families in their last moments of life. One soldiers' devotion to his children became a national cause celebre' in 1863: In the battle of Gettysburg, more than 17,000 Union soldiers fell, killed or wounded, during three days of fighting. During a Union retreat, Sergeant Humiston fell, and in his last moments, he took out a photograph of his three beloved children, and died with the photograph in his hand, presumably thinking of the children he would never see again. When the body was found, there was only one way to identify it: the photograph was published, and the "Children of the Battlefield" became one of the most famous photographs of the era. Ballads were written, funds raised, and the photograph became a symbol for the disaster visited upon innocent children by the war.

The original of this famous photograph of the three Humiston children was found clasped in their father's hands when his body was recovered from the battlefield.

Mrs. Loughborough related in her book an incident in which she and her daughter watched as a soldier friend carried away an unexploded artillery shell from their cave.

They heard an explosion, and then both witnessed Henry holding out his mangled arms—the hands torn and hanging from the bleeding, ghastly wrists—a fearful wound in his head—the blood pouring from his wounds. Shot, gasping, wild, he staggered around, crying piteously, "Where are you, boys? O boys, where are you?"...My little girl clung to my dress, saying, "O mamma, poor Henny's killed! Now he'll die, mamma."[75]

George Alfred Townsend was a well-known newspaper reporter who accompanied the Union army, reporting on his observations about the war. He described the aftermath of battles, and its effect on the civilian witnesses.

They [the soldiers] lay in their blankets upon the floors—pale, helpless...Such wrecks of power I never beheld....Only their rolling eyes distinguished them from mutilated corpses. One, who could speak, observing my pitiful glances toward his severed thigh, drew up his mouth and chin, and wept...in a corner clustered the terrified farmer and his family, vainly attempting to turn their eyes from the horrible spectacle. The farmer's wife had a baby at her breast, and its little blue eyes were straying over the room, half wonderingly, half delightedly. I thought, with a shudder, of babyhood thus surrounded, and how, in the long future, its first recollections of existence should be of booming guns and dying soldiers.[76]

The National Homestead of Gettysburg was just one of the many institutions set up to assist children who had been orphaned by the war.

The Benefits of War on American Life

Discussions of the impact of the Civil War very often dwell entirely on its devastating effects. These accounts provide an incomplete picture, for there were also beneficial effects of the war: The beneficial effects of the Civil War might be considered in three groups: 1) There were constitutional benefits of the war; as the country emerged united from a crisis more serious than any it had seen. 2) There were economic benefits; efforts to diversify the economy of the south out of agriculture and into manufacturing received a jump-start. 3) Modern feminists see a benefit to women as the war helped to reverse a trend to confine their public roles in life to the "domestic sphere." Thus it is attributed with reopening many career opportunities which had been closed to women in the early decades of the nineteenth century.

The women who had discussed property rights, and legal rights within their soldier's aid societies often became activists for the rights of women once the wartime duties no longer occupied their time.

However, there is one beneficial impact of the Civil War which overshadows constitutional, economic, and even sexual equality benefits. It is the fact that the Civil War became a catalyst for settling the issue of slavery.

Modern historians—and nineteenth century politicians—might assert that, from the outset, slavery was the main issue of the Civil War. Many Americans at the time would have disagreed. Lincoln's Emancipation Proclamation was not universally popular among Yankee soldiers.

> Lincoln's proclamation was not very well received by this portion of the army, they holding that it has come down to be a nigger war, fighting for the Blacks etc. But as you say in a former letter, if it only finishes this rebellion, sends every northern soldier to his home to follow his peaceful occupation, "The means will justify the end."[77]

Others saw the wisdom in Lincoln's actions

> If McClellan gets the reins he will have peace sooner than Abe, but by letting them have their slaves. Then we can fight them again in about ten years. But let Old Abe settle it, and it is always settled, is my opinion of the matter.[78]

By the time of the Civil War, the issue of slavery—its expansion and elimination—had been a prominent political issue for several decades. Various attempts were proposed—and opposed —to limit slavery. In the Presidential election of 1856, Republican candidate John C. Fremont ran on an anti-slavery platform that led the south to threaten to secede if he were elected. The threat helped to ensure Fremont's defeat. Instead, Buchanan was elected, and the slavery issue festered for another four years. During the campaign of 1860, southerners, encouraged by the campaign rhetoric of Democratic candidate Stephen A. Douglas, renewed their threat. Voters elected Abraham Lincoln anyway. Stephen A. Douglas was relegated—literally and figuratively—to holding Lincoln's hat.[79]

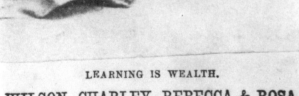

LEARNING IS WEALTH.

WILSON, CHARLEY, REBECCA & ROSA.

After the war, visual images of freed slave children—particularly those with light skin colors—were published and sold to raise money for various organizations and schools.

This photograph was taken on a cotton plantation on the sea islands off the Carolina coast. The U.S. Army experimented with hiring freedmen to work the cotton fields on a cooperative basis, in the belief that the land would be divided among the workers. Their efforts and organization were aborted when the government decided that the land would be returned to its former owners after the war.

In 1861, Lincoln named Fremont to command of the Western Department, and Fremont issued an emancipation proclamation freeing the slaves in that district. Lincoln rescinded the order as being untimely. In April of the following year, Lincoln signed into law a Congressional Act to free all slaves in the District of Columbia (and to compensate the owners of those slaves). The time was ripe for action, but Lincoln wanted to wait for a northern victory before taking further action on the issue. After the Battle of Antietam in September of 1862, Lincoln announced his Emancipation Proclamation which was to go into effect the following January. The Proclamation freed slaves in all states still in revolt as of January 1, 1863.

Few had expected Lincoln to immediately free all the slaves in America; for the sake of the economy if for no other reason. Even those who sought to limit slavery often found that their economic situations depended on the products of slave labor. One of the largest American industries in the northeast was the textile industry, which relied on the cotton produced by slave labor. One of the markets for American "factory cloth" was the southern market, where these cheap fabrics were used to clothe slaves. Like modern Americans, politicians in the mid-nineteenth century had to temper desirable goals against the potential for lost jobs and a depressed economy. However, there were arguments more compelling than economic ones.

Those who advocated the abolition of slavery used reasoning which, to the mid-nineteenth century mind, transcended all other arguments:

1. Slavery was unethical.
2. Slavery violated the sanctity of the family.
3. Slavery permitted indulgence of other vices.

Discussions that slavery violated basic human dignity were far less common than these.

1. Slavery was unethical: The moral and ethical arguments against slavery were advocated by the many ministers who became prominent speakers on the topic. Two such ministers were Reverend Lyman Beecher and his son, Henry Ward. (Even as they and other ministers preached on the biblical verses which condemned slavery, there were equally authoritative ministers in the

71

south quoting biblical verses to show that slavery was condoned by God.)

Reverend Lyman Beecher had a daughter, sister to Henry Ward, who condensed some of the most compelling arguments against slavery into a best-selling novel, *Uncle Tom's Cabin*, which did much to sway public opinion. (Southerners pointed out—with little effect—that all the worst villains in Harriet Beecher Stowe's book were displaced northerners, and that the book was, after all, fiction.)

2. Slavery violated the sanctity of the family: Abolitionists emphasized that slavery violated the sanctity of the family, black and white. They cited examples of slave families which had been broken up and various members sold off. (Southerners argued that slaves were seldom sold away from their families unless they misbehaved so badly that they caused disruption to the entire community.)

3. Slavery permitted indulgence of other vices (such as lying, and gambling): Abolitionists published numerous tragic accounts in which the pleasures of the master led to the separation of slave families for purely economic reasons, as when slaves were sold to pay gambling debts. (Southerners countered that the slaves became a part of their own families, and were in fact less likely to be separated than northern "wage slaves" who could be fired from their jobs at the whim of a manager or foreman.)

Finally, anti-slave literature often alluded to the mixed-race children which resulted from sexual alliances between masters and slaves.

Photographs of Caucasian-looking slave children were published and sold during and after the war to raise money for various causes. These photographs were powerful images.

Catherine Lawrence, who left school when she was orphaned at the age of 13, participated in the Civil War as a hospital administrator. At the end of the war, she adopted a former slave child of mixed parentage. Ms. Lawrence later wrote in her memoirs that her daughter, Virginia, should be baptized by none other than Henry Ward Beecher himself. The Reverend Beecher obliged

The Reverend Henry Ward Beecher, brother to Harriet Beecher Stowe, and son of the Reverend Lyman Beecher.

Fannie Virginia Casseopia Lawrence was one of the emancipated slave children whose picture was mass-produced and sold. Mrs. Lawrence does not mention in her diary if Fannie ever received any of the proceeds.

The armies were authorized to hire women to do laundry at locations in and near semi-permanent camps. It would appear that everyone in site has used the photograph as an excuse to take a break from their work.

and gave a stirring sermon. During the church service, the Reverend Beecher took up a collection for the education of the child, a collection rumored to total $2500.[80]

The various arguments against slavery received much publicity. The idea that slavery should be entirely abolished—regardless of the economic impact—moved from the lunatic fringe to the mainstream of public opinion in many areas of the north. As with the supporters of many popular causes, those who advocated the abolition of slavery did not present an entirely united front, and they did not necessarily advocate equality for blacks and whites.

Frederick Douglass had been born a slave on the Wye Plantation in Maryland. He had run away, traveled north, and obtained an education. Like few other blacks, he was admitted into northern social circles, and became an effective speaker for the cause of abolition.

During a trip to Europe, English supporters of Douglass raised money to purchase Douglass' freedom. Abolitionists in America were divided on the propriety of the purchase. Did it acknowledge that slave holders ought to be compensated? Did it make Douglass a less effective speaker that there was no danger he would be seized and returned to his master? Douglass himself noted that "the purchase of legal freedom [ought not be confused] with abstract right and natural freedom."[81]

One scheme supported by some abolitionists involved sending the freed slaves back to Africa or Liberia. Some blacks did, indeed, emigrate to Africa. In her childhood diary of Village Life in America, Carolyn Cowles Richmond reported that the black barber in her town had moved to Liberia. With the exception of noting that she read the Emancipation Proclamation, this cousin of Harriet Beecher Stowe never again mentioned blacks or slavery in her twenty-year diary.

It may not be by oversight that Carolyn neglected to mention the free blacks in her account of village life in New York state; there may have been no other blacks in her world.

The 1860 census of population of the nineteen non-slave states and 7 territories included 18.9 million whites and 237,000 free blacks.[82]

There was one free black for about every 80 whites. Many whites in the north grew up without ever knowing a free black. Indeed, there are numerous accounts of

Union soldiers—and civilians—who first encountered blacks when they invaded the south. The following is an excerpt from a letter Ruthie Osgood (who told about the man falling on the ice) wrote to her brother, Charlie Osgood, who was serving in the 1st Massachusetts Heavy Artillery.

> When Dr. N___ and Dr. H___ came home they brought darkies with them. How I wish you had brought one to me to wait upon me. How I should like it.[83]

Southerners were more universally familiar with blacks. In the 1860 census the population in the fifteen slave-holding states included 8.04 million whites, 3.9 million slaves, and 251,000 free blacks. The ratio of whites to free blacks was one free black for every 32 whites.[84] The majority of whites in the southern states owned no slaves, but had seen and knew blacks personally. Whites in the south were familiar with slaves who earned wages; owners of slaves often rented or loaned them out, collecting all or a portion of their wages.

The southern and northern attitudes toward blacks are reflected in the military processes and procedures. In the south, black slaves sometimes accompanied their masters when they joined the military. Some were carried on the company roles, and functioned as company cooks, teamsters, or servants.

At the outset of the war, blacks were not permitted to enlist in the U.S. military. When they were permitted to enlist, they were segregated into "colored" regiments, were led by white officers, and were offered lower pay than the white soldiers. The pay dispute was ultimately satisfied, but regiments remained segregated by race into the twentieth century.

Some northern soldiers were not entirely enthusiastic about the prospect of fighting alongside the colored troops. Hermon Clarke was a soldier who was perfectly willing to fight with black soldiers—as long as they were paid less than him.

Army teamsters at Cobb Hill, Virginia. Blacks who worked for the U.S. Army sometimes received cast-off uniforms and pay that was less than that of whites in similar positions.

...And in regard to hiring Negro soldiers I don't know a man so fond of soldiering that he is not willing to let the Negroes have the honors if they want them at $7 per month. And every one who has ever seen them acknowledges that they are the soldiers for this climate.[85]

Most, who saw the black troops fight came to admire them. The following quote is from the same soldier that wrote the one above.

...There are three colored regiments on the island, and they do good work. They fight well and do more fatigue duty than any white can. I am willing to let them fight and dig if they will....[86]

George W. Childs responded to critics of the colored troops in his 1863 publication, Light and Dark of the Rebellion. He entitled one chapter of his book "African Troops—The Future Armies of the Republic."

Those who have declaimed loudest against the employment of negro troops have shown a lamentable amount of ignorance, and an equally lamentable lack of common sense.[87]

He then details the valuable service blacks provided to armies in the Revolution, War of 1812, and the French-and-Indian wars. He closes the chapter with a prediction:

Our standing army will ultimately be made up chiefly of emancipated negroes; so will our navy; and they will in time make such a military and maritime force as never has been seen....The African race emancipated will hereafter constitute the great body-guard of the Union.[88]

The abolitionist Frederick Douglass was an advocate of permitting blacks to fight, and two of his sons joined the military. One of them was promoted to the position of Sergeant Major. He and his regiment, the 54th Massachusetts, made the gallant charge at the Battle of Fort Wagner, SC.

The soldiers who fought in the military were not the only blacks who performed brave acts during the war. There was, for example, Robert Smalls.[89] By way of background, Robert's mother, Lizzie, was a slave who led the sort of life which southerners would long cite as an example of the closeness between slave and mistress. Lizzie spent her early childhood on one of the sea islands plantations. Lizzie's mistress visited only occasionally, (as at Christmas to distribute oranges). As a young girl, Lizzie impressed her mistress, who brought her to the town home in Beaufort, that Lizzie might become a house servant. Lizzie grew up in service to her mistress, in the relatively comfortable surroundings of Beaufort. She bore a son, whom she named Robert Smalls. Lizzie never forgot her relatives on the sea islands plantations,

and raised her son to be aware of all aspects of slavery. Lizzie grew very close to her mistress, and during the Civil War, when Lizzie had an opportunity to escape to areas occupied by Union troops, she instead stayed with her mistress. After the war, Lizzie continued to care for her mistress until the older woman died.

Lizzie's son, Robert Smalls, led a very different life. When Robert was a young man, he began to show signs of rebelliousness. With Lizzie's concurrence (perhaps at her suggestion), he was permitted to move to Charleston, where he tried his hand at various trades. It was not an altruistic act by Robert's master; he was required to send to his master a good portion of his earnings. (For cash-strapped slaveholders, renting out slaves or permitting them to work for wages, was a relatively common source of additional income. Aside from a familiarity with free blacks, this practice is one of the reasons southerners were accustomed to blacks who worked for wages.)

Ultimately, Smalls became a worker on a steamboat known as the *Planter*, transporting cotton for his employer. This is the job which Smalls held during the first part of the Civil War. The *Planter* operated in and around Charleston Harbor, where Smalls became familiar with the signs and signals exchanged between Confederate vessels and the forts which guarded the harbor. When Robert saw an opportunity to escape from slavery, he made a different choice than his mother had made.

One night, when the white officers were ashore at a party, Smalls and his fellow slaves picked up their families, and steamed out of Charleston Harbor, exchanging appropriate signs with the Confederate forts which guarded the harbor. Smalls sailed up to the Union fleet, white sheets flying, and surrendered the *Planter*. It was an act which captured the imagination of northerners. Newspapers throughout the U.S. celebrated this moral victory that a slave had outsmarted the Confederate defenses. Smalls was sent to Washington to meet with President Lincoln and Secretary of War Stanton that he might encourage them to allow blacks to enlist in the military.

Through the rest of the war, Smalls worked for the U.S. Army on the *Planter*, eventually rising to a position as Captain of the boat. All was not smooth sailing. He endured the frustration of working under cowardly officers, and of being asked, even ordered, to abandon his beloved vessel. When Smalls took the *Planter* to Philadelphia for much-needed repairs, he was greeted as a celebrity by some, but he was still asked to move to the back of the trolley car.[90]

Asked to speak at public events, Smalls spoke on the importance of education. After the war, he returned to Beaufort and purchased, at a tax sale, the town home which had been his master's. Smalls and his family—along with Lizzie and her mistress—lived in the house after the war.

Smalls' story is far from ordinary, yet his determination to do right by his family, his advocacy of education, and his determination to live in peace with whites—even with the woman who kept him and his mother enslaved—mirror the experiences of thousands of other freedmen.

This is the only known war-time or pre-war photograph of Robert Smalls, escaped slave, captain of the **Planter,** *and South Carolina Congressman. In 1976, a monument to Robert Smalls was erected, bearing as its inscription, a quotation from Smalls:*

> *My race needs no special defense, for the past history of them in this country proves them to be the equal of any people anywhere. All they need is an equal chance in the battle of life—Robert Smalls November 1, 1895.*

Chapter VI
The End

And then came the end. Four years—almost to the day—after the firing on Fort Sumter, General Robert E. Lee surrendered, followed by General Johnston.

Mrs. Loughborough wrote a tribute to the men who fought at Vicksburg, but her comments are relevant to all who fought in the war:

> Words cannot express the wonder and admiration excited in [my] mind by the conduct of those brave men...how they endured with unflinching courage, the shower of ball and shell, how they confronted the foe with undaunted resolution, closing the ranks steadily as their comrades fell by hundreds about them; how they endured with steadfast perseverance, the hunger, the wet, the privation; ...and when the forlorn hope wavered and the flag was pulled down, how the dauntless faces paled before defeat as they had never paled before a foe.[91]

In the north, there was jubilation and celebration. Most were confident that the country could be reunited, although they did not always agree on strategies for accomplishing this goal. In various newspapers, editorials were printed urging leniency. Hub maker/debater/soldier Lester Frank Ward responded in a letter to the editor of the Washington Daily National Republican,

> We recognize the entire propriety and chivalry of General Grant's terms, offered as a conquering warrior, but we deny that the people, much less the soldiers, will be at all satisfied to see this wronged, defied, insulted and assailed nation grant a free pardon to those ineffable scoundrels who have grasped at its throat and stabbed at its heart....If the nation's statesmen cannot perceive this, its soldiers can.[92]

He signed the letter: "One Who Has Bled to Punish the Traitors."

While Union soldiers gathered in Washington, DC, for a magnificent victory parade, southern soldiers were left to walk home however they might, and rebuild lives in a shattered economy. At least they had the comfort that the President seemed a reasonable man, and if the reunion was to be accomplished "with malice toward none, and charity toward all," perhaps there was hope for the future.

Abraham Lincoln was assassinated just after the surrender, and the nation was shocked to find that their national hero had been slain by a national celebrity, a member of a family of famous actors. It was truly a turning point in American history, for many consider the Reconstruction era to have changed the period after the war to one of oppression rather than the rebuilding which Lincoln advocated.

For hundreds of thousands of freedmen, new freedom meant new and difficult decisions. It was widely recognized that education was a key to social and economic success. Freedman's schools were opened all over the south, often taught by young women from the north. These young women followed in the footsteps of the Quaker schoolmistresses who had been teaching freedmen on the sea islands since early in the war. Robert Smalls purchased at least one house which he turned over to be a school for children of his race. He was not alone in his efforts.

Susie King Taylor had been a slave on the sea islands, much like Smalls' own mother. After the war, Susie opened a school in Savannah. When the government opened free schools, Susie turned to domestic work.[93] She was not alone in her new occupation. The months and years after the war were not easy ones for anyone in the south. Blacks found that they were permitted to work in fewer occupations than before the war. Whites who had found it inconvenient to live under military rule during the war endured that rule for a decade more. Governors were sent into the states by the federal government, and those (like Winfield Scott Hancock) who tried to re-enfranchise the Confederate governments, were replaced.

Slowly, life returned to new definitions of "normal." In both the north and the south, some families waited months or years before their soldiers returned. One family mourned for five years, and then learned that their soldier was laying—alive—in a hospital not so very far away.[94] Others waited years, never hearing, never know-ing, if the soldier died in battle and was buried in an unmarked grave somewhere. Families mourned, and added these adult men to the family members they would see again in heaven. As individuals, and as a nation, Americans pulled back together under a single federal government.

The degree to which soldiers of north and south were able to put differences behind them, and reunite as brothers is unique in history. As George Childs noted in his book about the war,

> Anybody can be brave in battle under a good leader; but he alone is the real hero who can be brave when the battle is over.[95]

The success of these Americans in putting their hostilities behind them is a further tribute to their Judeo-Christian ethics, which had taught them that in the great scheme of things, they were brothers all along.

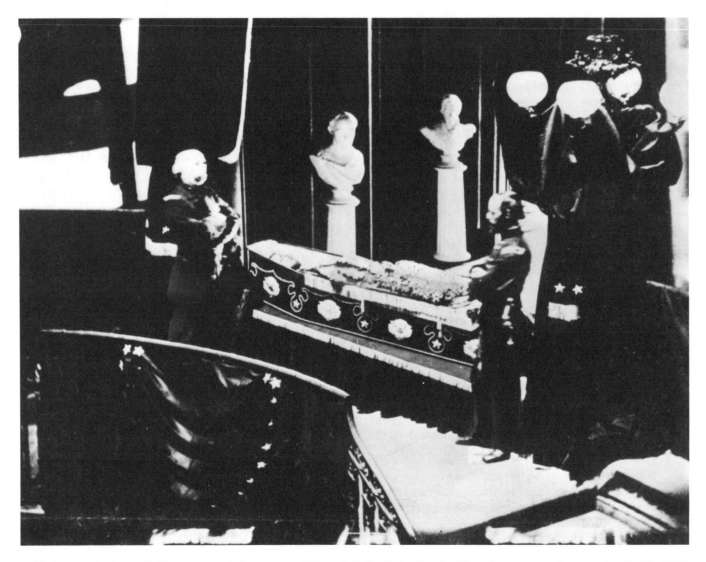

This image is the only known surviving view of Lincoln's body in death. The photo was taken on April 24, 1865. (Illinois State Historical Society)

In this pair of pictures, the elderly couple hold a small bouquet of flowers, and look into the camera with more than a trace of sadness.

In his 1863 publication, George Childs correctly predicted the outcome of the Civil War; and that the nation would be stronger for having endured it.

> There is no better way to test the integrity and power of a man or a commonwealth than to watch them in periods of trouble....Neither men nor nations ever develop their native characteristics in times of florid prosperity....It is only when the storm comes that the individual, the oak, the ship, or the community show their real strength....[96]

Men who were disabled by the war sometimes received pensions from the U.S. government, or (in the south) from their state governments. Family members did not always receive assistance even when the head of the household had been disabled in service to his country.

A Commentary on Sources

Those who study the Civil War are fortunate to have access to a vast storehouse of visual information. This war took place at a crossroads in history: it was the first war to take place after the advent of widespread literacy, and it was the last great American war before the military began censoring the information soldiers were permitted to send home. Written correspondence was a national pastime.

This was also the first great war to take place after photography became widely available. Although a relatively new science, photography had become immensely popular. Nearly every town in America could boast a photographer. Some photographers had visited the battlefields of the Crimea in the 1850s, but the extent to which photography was used in the Civil War changed the media coverage of war for all time.

The Americans who lived at the time of the Civil War often commented on the importance of photographs in their lives:

> And in the hospital wards, men...were talking of battles, prisoners, and captors, when each...took out pictures of innocent babes, little children, and wives, to show each other, all feeling a sympathy and interest in the unknown faces. Verily, war is a species of passionate insanity.[97]

Many of the photographic images carried by soldiers were albumen paper photographs commonly known as "cartes" or "cartes de visite." These photographs were printed as positive images on paper from glass negatives. As such, they were more easily transported and took up less space than the heavier, glass ambrotypes and daguerreotypes hich were kept in hard cases. The negatives used to produce cartes could be used to print multiple copies of the photographs, making cartes far more affordable than "hard" images. An American of even modest means could have his or her photograph made and purchase copies to distribute to friends and families.

Filling the family photograph album was a national pastime.

This man holds in his hand one of the small, paper cartes de visite photographs.

Soldiers had become familiar with these photographs before they went to war. Throughout the nation, families gathered in the evening and spent hours arranging and re-arranging photographs in the "family album." Stories were told about the friends and relatives pictured, ensuring that children in mid-nineteenth century knew as much about their own families as modern children know about fictional families of television. Filling the album was very much a goal, and lithographs of political figures or objects d'art could be purchased, thus making the albums primers in art and history, as well as genealogy.

Ruthie Osgood, for example, wrote her brother Charlie bi-weekly while he was away at war. In her letters, she seldom failed to mention this national pastime:

> This photo I send you [of Fan] is not mine. It belongs to Annie Fifield....So you must be careful of it and send it back as soon as you have seen enough of her. Sallie Burnham sent me a splendid one of herself a week or two ago....I am getting my Album filled up fast.[98]

Charlie must have valued Ruthie's letters, for he found a way to store the letters, after the war preserving them with other documents from his military service.

Charlie was not alone in his effort to preserve memoirs of his experiences. This war took place in an era in which memories of past events were treasured nearly as much as plans for the future. Those who lived through the Civil War, and those who came after retained letters like Charlie's among their family papers. Thus the letters, the journals and the photographs produced during the period were generally preserved, and many have survived to this day. Henry Cabot Lodge explained his decision to publish his boyhood remembrances of the war with a statement that reflected the attitude of many Americans:

> ...[I]t has seemed to me that...[even minor] impressions...are not without importance, because everything which may serve to explain or characterize or illustrate a struggle so momentous ought to have some value to those of the future who would seek the truth about the past.[99]

Memoirs, letters, biographies, and photographs from the mid-nineteenth century were the sources used in preparing this booklet. These sources of information are located at institutions such as the Library of Congress, the National Archives and the United States Army Military History Institute. Others are being preserved in the possession of private collectors.

Charles Osgood
In 1864, Osgood was shot in the head, losing one eye and part of the bridge of his nose. He survived, and after a stay in Annapolis hospitals, continued his military service as a clerk for the army, wearing a patch over his empty eye socket.

Endnotes

[1] All quotes in the Preface are from A Lady of Virginia (pseudonym for Judith White Brockenbrough McGuire), *The Diary of a Southern Refugee, During the War*. New York: E.J. Hale & Son, 1867, pp. 351-360.

[2] Letter from Ruthie to Charlie Osgood, Portsmouth, Massachusetts, January 17, 1864.

[3] Bernhard J. Stern, editor, *Young Ward's Diary*. New York: G.P. Putnam's Sons, 1935, pp. 51, 58, 63.

[4] Stern, p. 8.

[5] Stern, p. 9.

[6] Dinah Maria Muloch Craig, *A Woman's Thoughts about Women*. New York: Rudd & Carleton, 1859, pp. 67-68.

[7] Lucy Larcom, *A New England Girlhood: Outlined from Memory*. Boston: Houghton Mifflin Company, 1889, p. 199.

[8] To Addie From Cary (undated autograph in Addie Kimball's 1861 autograph album).

[9] Stern, p. 33.

[10] Garrett, Dick and Fitzgerald, *Inquire Within for Anything you Want to Know, or Over Three Thousand Seven Hundred Facts Worth Knowing*. New York: Dick and Fitzgerald, 1856, p. 237.

[11] O.E. Rolvaag, "The Heart That Dared Not Let in the Sun," quoted in *The Private Side of American History: Readings in Everyday Life*. Vol. I, to 1877 ed. by Gary B. Nash. New York: Harcourt Brace Jovanovich, Inc., 1975, pp. 332-350.

[12] Mary H. and Dallas M. Lancaster, *The Civil War Diary of Anne S. Frobel of Wilton Hill in Virginia*. Birmingham, AL: Birmingham Printing & Publishing Co., 1986, p. 91.

[13] A Grandmother, *Advice to Young Mothers on the Physical Education of Children*. Boston: Hilliard, Gray & Co., 1833, pp. 55-56.

[14] To the best of the author's knowledge, the originator of this analogy was Mark Greenough, Living History Associates, Richmond, Va.

[15] Miss Lucy S.V. King, (Untitled) letter published in *Confederate Veteran Magazine*. North Carolina: Broadfoot, Volume XXXVIII, p. 375. (Originally published by the Sons of Confederate Veterans, 1926.)

[16] Catherine S. Lawrence, *Sketch of life and Labors of Miss Catherine S. Lawrence*. Albany, NY: James B. Lyon, 1896, p. 19.

[17] Henry L. Swint, editor, *Dear Ones At Home, Letters from Contraband Camps*. Nashville, TN: Vanderbilt University Press, 1966, p. 123.

[18] This theory was tested by typing into a Macintosh computer the first and last lessons from readers published for various grade levels. Microsoft Word software version 5.0 program using CorrectText by Houghton Mifflin (1991) was used to estimate the years of education needed to comprehend the text. Among the most striking results was the test performed on a "fifth reader." The first lesson was grade 7.6, and the last lesson was grade 18.2.

[19] Caroline Cowles Richards, *Village Life in America, 1852-1872*. New York: Henry Holt and Company, 1913, p. 107.

[20] A similar movement in the early decades had all but died out, and so this trend was actually a re-birth of an earlier movement. It was especially popular in communities with Germanic roots.

[21] Fanny Fern, *Fern Leaves from Fanny's Port-Folio*. Cincinnati: Henry W. Derby, 1853, p. 282.

[22] Stern, p. 113.

[23] A transcript of this May 18, 1863, letter is located in Ward's pension file at the National Archives.

[24] E.W. Locke, *Three Years in Camp and Hospital*. Boston: George D. Russell & Co., 1871, pp. 145-146.

[25] Margaret Brobst Roth, *Well Mary, Civil War Letters of a Wisconsin Volunteer*. Madison, WI: University of Wisconsin Press, 1960, p. 15.

[26] Philip Dunaway and Mel Evans, *A Treasury of the World's Greatest Diaries*, Garden City, NY: Doubleday & Co., Inc., 1957, p. 251.

[27] November 20, 1862, letter from John French White to his wife, "Mattie." The John French White letters are in the collection of the Virginia Historical Society, Richmond, VA.

[28] Parthenia Antoinette Hague, *A Blockaded Family: Life in Southern Alabama During the Civil War*. Boston: Houghton, Mifflin and Co., 1888, p. 14.

[29] George W. Childs, *The Light and Dark of the Rebellion*, Philadelphia: George W. Childs, 1863, p. 170.

[30] Recommendation letter to Charles Fisher, July 18, 1860. Sympathy letter from Charles Fisher to the widow White, January 6, 1861. Request for free passage for the corpse, January 5th, 1861.

[31] Stern, p. 145.

[32] November 20, 1862, letter from John French White to his wife, "Mattie." The John French White letters are in the collection of the Virginia Historical Society, Richmond, VA.

[33] Ethel Alice Hurn, *Wisconsin History Commission. Original Papers No. 6, Wisconsin Women in the War Between the States*, Wisconsin. Wisconsin History Commission, 1911. Quoted from H.W. Rood, Company E, and the Twelfth Wisconsin in the War for the Union (Milwaukee, 1893), p. 3.

[34] Autograph album of Mildred Reynolds Saffold, 1860-1861. Private Collection.

[35] Richards, p. 131.

[36] Mary Phelan Watt, "Alabama in the War," *Confederate Veteran Magazine*. North Carolina: Broadfoot, Volume XXIV, p. 225.

[37] Mrs. Fannie A. Beers, Memories, *A Record of Personal Experience and Adventure During Four Years of War*. Time Life, 1985, p. 230. (Originally published by J.B. Lippincott Company, 1888.)

[38] Roth, p. 142.

[39] Anonymous, Letters section, *Confederate Veteran Magazine*, North Carolina: Broadfoot, Vol. XXVIII, p. 375.

[40] Hague, p. 14.

[41] General Robert E. Lee, General Order No. 9, Army of Northern Virginia, April 10, 1865.

[42] Richard D. Goff, Confederate Supply. Durham, NC: Duke University Press, 1969, Introductory paragraphs.

[43] "Annual Report, Quartermaster Department, fiscal year ending 6/30/62," *Official Records, War of the Rebellion*. Series III, Vol. II, p. 804.

[44] W.E. Woodward, *A New American History*. New York: Garden City Publishing Co., 1938, p. 541.

[45] Henry Cabot Lodge, *Early memories*. New York: Charles Scribner's Sons, 1913, p. 120.

[46] Sarah M. Broadhead, *The Diary of a Lady of Gettysburg, Pennsylvania*. Hershey, PA: Gary T. Hawbaker, 1990.

[47] Ruth L. Silliker, editor, *The Rebel Yell & the Yankee Hurrah: The Civil War Journal of a Maine Volunteer*. Camden, ME, Down East Books, 1985, pp. 29-30.

[48] Broadhead, p. 21.

[49] Locke, p. 186.

[50] Sylvia G.L. Dannett, *Noble Women of the North*. New York: Thomas Yoseloff, 1959, pp. 81-82.

[51] Locke, p. iii.

[52] Note from Harriet P. Dame, January 4, 1886. Transcription of note in MOLLUS collection scrapbook. Washington, DC, January 4, 1886.

[53] Donald E. Press, "South of the Avenue," *Records of the Columbia Historical Society of Washington, D.C.* Vol. 51, Charlottesville: University Press of Virginia, 1984, pp. 55-56.

[54] Lee C. Drickamer and Karen D. Drickamer, *Fort Lyon to Harper's Ferry, On the Border of North and South with Ramblin Jour*. Shippensburg, PA: White Mane Publishing Co., Inc., 1987, p. 215.

[55] Locke pp. 181-182.

[56] Dinah Maria Muloch Craig. *A Life for a Life*. London: Hust and Blackett, 1861, p. 1.

[57] Philip Dunaway, "War—Without Hope, Without Victory," *The World's Greatest Diaries*, p. 248.

[58] Daniel Aaron, *The Hales and the Great Rebellion, Letters: 1861-1865*. Northampton, MA: Smith College, 1966, p. 38.

[59] Roth, p. 46.

[60] John Gallatin Paxton, *The Civil War Letters of General Frank Bull Paxton, A Lieutenant of Lee and Jackson*. Hillsboro, TX: Hill Jr. College Press, 1978, pp. 4, 6, 8, 9.

[61] Harry F. Jackson and Thomas F. O'Donnell, *Back Home in Oneida. Hermon Clarke and his Letters*. Syracuse, NY: Syracuse University Press, 1965, p. 156.

[62] Lancaster, p. 46.

[63] Drickamer, pp. 179-182.

[64] Lancaster, pp. 16-17.

[65] Locke, p. 169.

[66] Lancaster, p. 22, 27, 48.

[67] Swint, p. 142.

[68] Swint, pp. 11-12. She reports that the conversation continued with a play on words. "Who was the author of those lines? I inquired. I 'offers' em to you now, myself, he replied."

[69] Hague pp. 48-49.

[70] Hague pp. 99-100.

[71] Mrs. James M. Loughborough, *My Cave Life in Vicksburg, with Letters of Trial and Travel*. Spartanburg, SC: The Reprint Company, 1976, p. 137 [originally published by Kellogg Print Co., Little Rock, AR, 1882].

[72] Letter from John French White to his wife, Mattie, May 19, 1862. The letter is in the collection of the Virginia Historical Society, Richmond, Va.

[73] John French White Letter, March 21, 1863.

[74] Jackson, p. 177.

[75] Loughborough p. 129.

[76] George Alffred Townsend, *Campaigns of a Non-Combatant*. New York: Blelock & Company, 1866, pp. 131-132.

[77] Carl E. Hatch, editor, *Dearest Susie*. New York: Exposition Press, 1971, p. 37.

[78] Roth, p. 92.

[79] Irving Stone, *They Also Ran*. New York: Doubleday & Co., 1966, p. 239.

[80] Lawrence, p. 166. She further noted that, despite repeated appeals to the Reverend Beecher, she never received a penny of the money commenting "I was deaconed out of it."

[81] Aileen S. Draditor, *Means and Ends in American Abolitionism*. New York: Pantheon Books, 1969, p. 221.

[82] Kennedy, p. 5.

[83] Ruthie to Charlie Osgood, Salisbury, Mass., Sept. 20, 1863.

[84] Kennedy, p. 5.

[85] Jackson, p. 116.

[86] Jackson, p. 100.

[87] Childs, p. 198.

[88] Childs, pp. 205-207.

[89] Some of the information on Robert Smalls and his mother is from the family archives and oral history, as relayed by Mrs. Janet D. Nash.

[90] It was the middle of a rainstorm, and Smalls' response was that he would rather get off the trolley than move from the covered front to the uncovered back portion of the trolley. The incident received much publicity in Philadelphia newspapers at the time.

[91] Loughborough, p. viii.

[92] Stern, p. 167.

[93] Eve Merriam, editor, *Growing Up Female in America: Ten Lives*. New York: Dell Publishing Co., 1971, p. 198.

[94] I am indebted to Jeff Copeland for this piece of history from his Tennessee family.

[95] Childs, p. 12. Childs attributes this quote to "The great Prince Eugene."

[96] Childs, p. 303.

[97] Loughborough, p. 13.

[98] Ruthie to Charlie Osgood, Salisbury, Mass., Sept. 20, 1863.

[99] Lodge, p. 112.

Bibliography

Aaron, Daniel. *The Hales and the Great Rebellion, Letters: 1861-1865*. Northampton, MA: Smith College, 1966.

Baird, Nancy Chapalear. *Journals of Amanda Virginia Edmonds: Lass of the Mosby Confederacy, 1859-1867*. Stephens City, VA: Commercial Press, 1984.

Barton, George. *Angels of the Battlefield: A History of the Labors of the Catholic Sisterhoods in the Late Civil War*. Philadelphia: The Catholic Arat Publishing Company, 1897.

Beers, Mrs. Fannie A. *Memories: Record of Personal Experience and Adventure During Four Years of War*. Philadelphia: J. B. Lippincott Company, 1888. [Reprinted by Time Life, 1985.]

Broadhead, Sarah M. *Diary of a Lady of Gettysburg, Pennsylvania*. Hershey, PA: Gary T. Hawbaker, 1990.

Childs, George W. *The Light and Dark of the Rebellion*. Philadelphia: George W. Childs, 1863.

Craig, Dinah Maria Muloch. *A Life for a Life*. London: Hust and Blackett, 1861.

Craig, Dinah Maria Muloch. *A Woman's Thoughts about Women*. New York: Rudd & Carleton, 1859.

Dannett, Sylvia G. L. *Noble Women of the North*. New York: Thomas Yoseloff, 1959.

Dannett, Sylvia G. L. and Katharine M. Jones. *Our Women of the Sixties*. Washington, D.C.: U.S. Civil War Centennial Commission, 1963.

Dawson, Sarah Morgan. *A Confederate Girl's Diary*. Boston: Houghton Mifflin Company, 1913.

Draditor, Aileen S. *Means and Ends in American Abolitionism*. New York: Pantheon Books, 1969.

Drickamer, Lee C. and Karen D. Drickamer. *Fort Lyon to Harper's Ferry, On the Border of North and South with Rambling Jour*. Shippensburg, PA: White Mane Publishing Co., Inc., 1987.

Dunaway, Philip and Mel Evans. *A Treasury of the World's Great Diaries*. Garden City, NY: Doubleday & Company, Inc., 1957.

Fern, Fanny. *Fern Leaves from Fanny's Port-Folio*. Cincinnati: Henry W. Derby, 1853.

Garrett, Dick, and Fitzgerald. *Inquire Within for Anything you Want to Know, or Over Three Thousand Seven Hundred Facts Worth Knowing*. New York: Dick and Fitzgerald, 1856.

Goff, Richard D. *Confederate Supply*. Durham, NC: Duke University Press, 1969.

A Grandmother. *Advice to Young Mothers on the Physical Education of Children*. Boston: Hilliard, Gray & Co., 1833.

Hague, Parthenia Antoinette. *A Blockaded Family: Life in Southern Alabama During the Civil War*. Boston: Houghton, Mifflin and Company, 1888.

Harrison, Mrs. Carter H. *"Strange to Say—" Recollections of Persons and Events in New Orleans and Chicago*. Chicago: A. Kroch and Son, 1949.

Hatch, Carl E. *Dearest Susie: A Civil War Infantryman's Letters to His Sweetheart*. New York: Exposition Press, 1971.

Holliday, John Hampden. *Indianapolis and the Civil War*. Indianapolis: Indiana Historical Society, 1972.

Horrocks, James. *My Dear Parents: The Civil War Seen by an English Union Soldier*. New York: Harcourt Brace Jovanovich, 1982.

Hurn, Ethel Alice. *Wisconsin Women in the War Between the States, History Paper No. 6*. Wisconsin History Commission, May, 1911.

Jackson, Harry F. and Thomas F. O'Donnell. *Back Home in Oneida. Hermon Clarke and his Letters*. Syracuse, NY: Syracuse University Press, 1965.

Kimball, Addie. *Autograph Book 1861*. The book is in a private collection.

King, Miss Lucy S. V. "Letters" published in *Confederate Veteran Magazine*. North Carolina: Broadfoot, Volume XXXVIII.

Lancaster, Mary H. and Dallas M. Lancaster. *The Civil War Diary of Anne S. Frobel of Wilton Hill in Virginia*. Birmingham, AL: Birmingham Printing & Publishing Co., 1986.

Larcom, Lucy. *A New England Girlhood: Outlined from Memory*. Boston: Houghton Mifflin Company, 1889.

Lawrence, Catherine S. *Sketch of Life and Labors of Miss Catherine S. Lawrence*. Albany, NY: James B. Lyon, 1896.

Locke, E. W. *Three Years in Camp and Hospital*. Boston: George D. Russell & Co., 1871.

Lodge, Henry Cabot. *Early Memories*. New York: Charles Scribner's Sons, 1913.

Loughborough, Mrs. James M. *My Cave Life in Vicksburg, with Letters of Trial and Travel*. Little Rock, AR: Kellogg Print Co., 1882. [reprinted by The Reprint Company, Spartanburg, SC, 1976.

McGuire, Judith White (Brockenbrough). *The Diary of a Southern Refugee, During the War*. New York: E. J. Hale & Son, 1867.

Merriam, Eve, editor. *Growing Up Female in America: Ten Lives*. New York: Dell Publishing Company, 1971.

Morrow, Maud E. *Recollections of the Civil War*. Lockland, OH: John C. Morrow, 1901.

Paxton, John Gallatin, editor. *The Civil War Letters of General Frank "Bull" Paxton: A Lieutenant of Lee and Jackson*. Hillsboro, TX: Hill Jr. College Press, 1978.

Press, Donald E. "South of the Avenue," Records of the Columbia Historical Society of Washington, DC., Volume 51. Charlottesville, VA: University Press of Virginia, 1984.

Richards, Caroline Cowles. *Village Life in America. 1852-1872*. New York: Henry Holt and Company, 1913.

Rolvaag, O. E. "The Heart That Dared Not Let in the Sun," quoted in Nash, Gary B. *The Private Side of American History: Readings in Everyday Life*. Vol. I, to 1877. New York: Harcourt Brace Jovanovich, Inc., 1975. to 1877.

Roth, Margaret Brobst. *Well Mary, Civil War Letters of a Wisconsin Volunteer*. Madison, WI: University of Wisconsin Press, 1960.

Schlissel, Lillian. *Women's Diaries of the Westward Journey*. New York: Schocken Books, 1982.

Silliker, Ruth L., ed. *The Rebel Yell & the Yankee Hurrah: The Civil War Journal of a Maine Volunteer*. Camden, ME: Down East Books, 1985.

Smedes, Susan Dabney. *Memorials of a Southern Planter*. New York: Alfred A. Knopf, 1965.

Stern, Bernhard J., editor. *Young Ward's Diary: The Record of Lester Frank Ward*. New York: G. P. Putnam's Sons, 1935.

Stock, Maray Wright. *Shinplasters and Homespun: The Diary of Laura Nisbet Boykin*. Rockville, MD: Printer, Printex, 1975.

Stone, Irving. *They Also Ran*. New York: Exposition Press, 1971.

Swint, Henry L., editor. *Dear Ones at Home, Letters from Contraband Camps*. Nashville, TN: Vanderbilt University Press, 1966.

Taylor, Susie King. *Reminiscences of my Life in Camp with the 33rd U.S. Colored Troops, Late 1st South Carolina Volunteers*. Boston: Susie King Taylor, 1902. [Reprinted by Markus Wiener Publishing, 1988.]

Townsend, George Alfred. *Campaigns of a Non-Combatant, and his Romaunt Abroad During the War*. New York: Blelock & Company, 1866.

Watt, Mary Phelan. "Alabama in the War," *Confederate Veteran Magazine*. North Carolina: Broadfoot, Volume XXIV.

Woodward, W.E. *A New American History*. New York: Garden City Publishing Co., 1938.

Wright, Mrs. D. Giraud. *A Southern Girl in '61: The War-Time Memories of a Confederate Senator's Daughter*. New York: Doubleday, Page & Company, 1905.

Young, Agatha. *The Women and the Crisis: Women of the North in the Civil War*. New York: McDowell, Obolensky, 1959.

THOMAS PUBLICATIONS publishes books about the American Colonial era, the Revolutionary War, the Civil War, and other important topics. For a complete list of titles, please write to:

THOMAS PUBLICATIONS
P.O. Box 3031
Gettysburg, PA 17325